Bancroft of the
Bengal Horse Artillery

Staff Sergeant N. W. Banroft

Bancroft of the Bengal Horse Artillery

An Account of the
First Sikh War
1845-1846

N. W. Bancroft,

Bancroft of the Bengal Horse Artillery
by N. W. Bancroft,

First published under the title
From Recruit to Staff Sergeant
1885

Leonaur is an imprint
of Oakpast Ltd

Copyright in this form © 2008 Oakpast Ltd

ISBN: 978-1-84677-566-6 (hardcover)
ISBN: 978-1-84677-565-9 (softcover)

http://www.leonaur.com

Publisher's Notes

In the interests of authenticity, the spellings, grammar and place names used have been retained from the original editions.

The opinions of the authors represent a view of events in which he was a participant related from his own perspective,
as such the text is relevant as an historical document.

The views expressed in this book are not necessarily
those of the publisher.

Contents

Prefatory and Personal	7
Marching	15
Soldiering.	30
Moodkee	53
Ferozeshah.	64
Aliwal	82
Standing Camp	91
Sobraon	99
Quarters	113
Soldiering 2	118
Pay and Stoppages.	124
Appendix A	127
Appendix B.	132
Appendix C	135

CHAPTER 1.

Prefatory and Personal

So far as the writer has been able to ascertain (he writes under correction and gives the popular version), the first Commandant of the Horse Artillery of the Honourable East India Company, was Clement Brown, C. B. That officer was descended from an Irish family, and was appointed to a cadetship in 1783. He arrived in Bengal in July 1784, and was gazetted ensign of infantry on the establishment on 3rd February 1785. Owing to the great deficiency of officers in the Bengal Artillery about this time, a number were transferred from the infantry in 1788, and Ensign Brown was commissioned in the artillery as a Fireworker (that he was a fire-eater goes without saying), in the early part of 1789, and posted to the 1st company, 2nd battalion (3-23 R. A.). In January 1800, Lord Wellesley, being desirous of raising a troop of horse artillery (the first of that description of arm), Captain Brown was selected by him to superintend its formation.

A detachment of this troop, two guns, and a proportion of horses, was despatched to Egypt from India in 1801, but on the march across the desert, Captain Brown lost his horses from scarcity of water, and the guns were taken on by camels. In August 1802, Captain Brown and his men returned to Bengal. This troop is supposed to have been the origin of the first troop, first brigade, horse artillery, which was afterwards cut up (with exceptions hereinafter mentioned), in the retreat from Cabul in 1841-42.

About 1803 what was called the experimental brigade was formed, but not in time to share in any of the actions against the Mahrattas in that year. It was on the 7th October 1804, that the horse artillery guns were first unlimbered for action, under the command of Captain Brown, in front of an enemy, upon which occasion the despatch recording the action says that they "did the State good service." The subsequent services of the troop in this campaign need not be here detailed. The horse artillery was virtually a new arm in the service in warfare, and no doubt had its shortcomings, but the services of this battery in General Lake's pursuit of Holkar, &c, evince the care which Captain Brown must have bestowed upon his men and horses, and bear sufficient testimony to his excellence as as horse artillery officer.

He commanded this arm at the second siege of Bhurtpore in 1825, which he had also seen attacked in 1805, and for this and his other services he was, on the 26th December 1826, nominated a Companion of the Bath. In September 1831 he was appointed commandant of the regiment after a service of 48 years. In August 1836 he was placed upon the staff of the army as a Brigadier-General in command of the Benares division, and his promotion to the rank of major-general followed in January 1837. He died at Benares on the 24th of April 1838 in his 72nd year. He was warm-hearted and impulsive, like the generality of his countrymen, and though somewhat eccentric in his bounty in later years, ever liberal with his purse.

It was about October 1832 the writer first saw the brigadier commandant. It was at Chitpore Ghât, as it was then called, a few miles from Dum-Dum, where he had come to march into that station a troop of horse artillery (without guns or horses, having left them at Cawnpore), under the command of Lieutenants Grant and Henry Lawrence (afterwards the celebrated Sir Henry, who was killed at Lucknow in the mutiny), which had just landed from country boats;

their original boats, and every article the officers and men of the troop possessed, having been swept away in the cyclone of that year, which had unfortunately overtaken them on the passage downwards. It was the custom in those days, for troops of horse artillery marching from Dum-Dum to Cawnpore (the statutory first station up-country), to leave their horses and guns behind them to be taken up by the relieving troop on their arrival down-country, the progress to and fro not being made by road, but by the river, that "silent highway of waters." In consequence of their losses, the men of the troop were dressed like natives; which so excited the commiseration of the old commandant, that he shed bitter tears as he took his place at the head of the troop, and marched them, the band playing in front, into the barrack square of Dum-Dum.

It was some days, of course, before matters were settled, The troop just arrived had their uniform to receive, and to take over the horses and guns of the troop they were relieving, which, on making all over, took its departure for Cawnpore by the river route without the cyclone accompaniment.

So much for the regiment, now for the recruit: and as the generality of readers, if a man may judge by himself (and human nature is everywhere the same), are wishful to know something about the man who comes before them in the shape of an author (no matter on how small a scale), the writer of these lines makes a profound bow, and the following interesting announcement. It is not exactly a domestic occurrence, but it has a good deal to do (as will appear hereafter), with the birth of this little venture,

After the excitement had subsided attending the arrival and departure of the troops, the writer, a very small shaver, was attending the regimental school, which it was the brigadier's custom to visit regularly. On one of these visits the writer had been reported by a school-fellow (a girl, he believes, for girls are at the bottom of all mischief!), in some childish dispute, which report had found its way to the ears of the brigadier; and the writer's small cheeks tingled, and he saw a thousand stars with his little eyes, as the result of a smart slap on his cheek given by the hand of the brigadier himself, who believing in the offence alleged to have been committed by the writer, was thus administering reproof and correction, Whether a conviction of innocence or shame, or wounded self-pride was the cause need not be said, but the result was a fit of sobbing, so violent, that the brigadier became much affected, gave the writer a holiday, and ordered the schoolmaster to take him to the tailor's shop and there be measured for a suit of new clothes at his expense, as a compensation or *solatium* to his wounded feelings, which plaster had the effect of curing his complaint immediately.

In a few days the suit was ready (and in the possession of the writer, and he made up his small mind, that he would wait upon the brigadier at his own house (a large bungalow in Dum-Dum called Fairy Hall, which is still extant) to thank him for his present, and at the same time express his desire to become a soldier. He was only nine years of age, and you may imagine what a precocious youth, he must have been! Acting upon the resolution, and unaccompanied, the writer boldly attacked the brigadier in his hall, and experienced little difficulty in having his request granted. The old man kindly patted him on the shoulder, saying "Yes, my little man, you shall be a little soldier." On the following day he was "in orders," as it was called, and posted to the artillery band, on 1st February 1833.

Years rolled on, until at length on the 7th of December, in the year of Grace one thousand eight hundred and forty-one, when leather breeches and long boots, brass helmets with red horse-hair manes, and jackets with ninety buttons, or, by Our Lady a hundred, were the favourite dress of the Bengal Horse Artillery, who vaunted themselves, and with justice and reverence be it spoken, the finest specimens of that arm in the world; when shaven chins and upper lips, and mutton-chop whiskers (according to regulation) were the order of the day—the reader's very humble servant attained the mature age of 18 years, and his service began to count towards a pension; or, what was called in those days, his *man service* began to run. He was then stationed in Dum-Dum, which was still the headquarters of the artillery arm of the Honourable East India Company. The height of his ambition was then, and had long been, to become a horse-artilleryman. He had spent the whole nine long years of his boy service in the foot artillery (better known by the classical appellation of Old Fogs—an expression which stank in his nostrils, and was fraught with all sorts of ridiculous and disagreeable associations). Had spent these years, too, almost entirely under canvas; and if marching from one end of India to the other and back, could be said to be good training for a professional pedestrian, he was certainly entitled to set up in business as one on his own account, and make a good thing of it. For example, the writer's first march was from Dum Dum to Agra (at the age of twelve years) on the 5th of November 1835, which lasted three months, he walked all the way without a tot of grog,—no beer in those days; several men were flogged on this march for trifling offences. June 1837 at Agra he was on parade with the 4th Battalion Bengal Artillery when a Royal Salute of 21 guns was fired for Her Majesty the Queen succeeding to the throne. There is one incident which may be worth relating here. On the 22nd June 1897 he loaded and fired the first, gun of the Diamond Jubilee in Simla.

In June 1838 (in the monsoons) he marched from Agra on a campaign to Jodhpore. On the march we had no baker or butcher, and lived on *chappaties* (native cakes) and birds we shot for 21 days force marches, till we reached Nusseerabad.

It is an awful fact that when unexpectedly called to march against a rebellious fort at the hottest time of the year, four of our men were on the first and second day's march found dead from drunkenness, lying on the road, or having thrown themselves into wells.

Another occurrence, soon after the commencement of this march, we had halted on a Sunday, after the usual march, at a place called Uncha-Shehir, otherwise *Lall Sont.*

We had experienced much vexation from the indisposition of the towns people to furnish supplies, especially carts to convey lame and sick men. The flooded state of the country, and the rains which fell, kept the men constantly in wet clothes,—it was desirable to be always on the move, The town was of notoriously evil repute as a den of robbers. A zealous young subaltern of our party, highly indignant at the way we were treated, took a party of Europeans, (the writer being one of the number) to the town to enforce the necessary requisition. A rumour reached camp that the small party were surrounded there—some killed, and all in danger of being cut off. The assembly was sounded in camp, the writer at the time was bugler, he repeated the call. The remaining portion of the detachment left the camp under the officer commanding (the camp was left to the care of the lascars) at the double to rescue their comrades, but the detachment had not advanced very far before they met the writer's party returning and all safe.

The subaltern in charge of the party had penetrated into the town after it had become dark, leaving some men to keep possession of the gateway. They went under the walls of a lofty keep, and then after an altercation and an insulting answer from its walls, they attempted to drag away some carts and bullocks. In the act of doing this, a man rushed at the subaltern, pushed the writer aside as being below his notice, cutting right and left, and wounded him under the arm, the officer only saved his life by running the man through the body with his sword. The subaltern was a little above five feet high. He would not allow any men of the detachment to assist him. The detachment had no guns, neither were they furnished with fire arms, the only weapon of the men being a short sword and it blunt.

The whole of our little camp was thenceforth so excited that the commanding officer judged it best to strike the tents, and march away, taking our prisoners with us, they were forwarded on to the Resident at Jeypore, this ended our little affray with only one life lost. These solemn scenes together, with the misgivings incident, to young soldiers suddenly sent on active service for the first time, for we were led to expect a desperate resistance from the fort against which we were going (one of the strongest in India). The country we passed through was given up to lawlessness and bloodshed, victims of violence and avengers of blood met us at every step, "Yet" though strangers in the land, and a few in it, "He suffered no man to do us wrong, and reproved even kings for our sakes," Not only was the Rajah obliged to give up his fort without fighting; but other Rajahs, on our representations of the disorders in their territories, were called to account by our Government. Through some influence exerted, muskets and ammunition were obtained for our little band on our return march to Agra.

Having besides to convey old captured guns from the Ajmere Magazine, this, with the news now flying through India, of the fall of Ghuznee, and other successes in Afghanistan quite turned the tide of opinion so that our progress resembled a triumphant march; and even on approaching Uncha-Shehir, the one of our former misadventure, the inhabitants were ready to anticipate all our wishes, and showed us the utmost respect, they had even so feared our coming that they had propitiated their gods erecting two huge idols near the encamping ground. We were three months on this march back to Agra. Then we marched from Agra to Cawnpore, then back to Dum Dum in 1841, and of course had to walk every inch of the way further without a taste of grog.

But he had made up his mind that, if possible, he would cut the dismounted branch of the service, and if there was marching to be done, it should be either on a horse's back or on a gun-carriage. He had a soul above gutter-slapping, and set about having his desire gratified.

During the time his boy's service had been running he had not been idle. He had the proper complement of eyes, ears and hands, and young as he was, knew tolerably well how to use them—no bad accomplishment in those remote days when might was as often right as not. And he had often heard the old hands say in the barrack-room and the tent, that it was the worst thing in the world for a man to trust to a go-between or a deputy.

"Av yer warnt yer boots clainin;" said an old Irishman, grown grey in the service, "black 'em yerself! Yer sure they'll be done well; an iv yer warnt anything done fur ye, don't you be goin' about to understrappers, and this fellow an that chap, but go straight to the hid av the house!"

"Begorra!" said the old fellow, "I put no faith in detachments: thim is shaky more or less; but there's no mistake in hid-quarters!"

To apothegms such as these, the. writer did seriously incline, and guided and encouraged by his previous success with Brigadier Brown, and getting himself up regimentally with more than common care, he waited upon no less a personage than the then brigadier commandant of the artillery regiment, General Whish (Mooltan Whish he was called), and modestly preferred his request. It was kindly granted, and in a few days he found himself transferred to the second troop, first brigade, Horse Artillery, (now the C. C, R. H. A.) then stationed in Kurnal, in Upper India which involved the necessity of another three and a half months' promenading. In the meanwhile he was attached to the first troop, third brigade, Horse Artillery (Brind's troop), stationed at Dum-Dum, and which, it may be remarked, was the last troop of horse artillery destined to be stationed there. The reader is assured that there was no prouder man in India than the writer when the transfer was granted. His personal dignity was augmented; he seemed to breathe a higher and purer atmosphere: and there is no great harm in confessing (after all these years) in the language of the poetaster that he considered himself "no small potatoes!"

Chapter 2.

Marching

A very short, time after this the depressing intelligence reached Dum-Dum of the army in Cabul having been massacred, and on the 3rd of February 1842, Brinds's troop of Horse Artillery (first troop, third Brigade), marched from Dum-Dum to the Upper Provinces, taking with them the following recruits—50 for the horse artillery (the writer among the number; 100 for the foot artillery, and 400 for the 1st Bengal European Infantry Regiment (popularly known as the 1st Yeos), and jolly time's they were on that blessed march, wiling away the tedium of the marches by whistling, singing, cracking jokes, playing practical tricks, and all sorts of what was commonly called "divilment!" There was a very large contingent of Irishmen among the number, and the well-known tendency of the Hibernian mind to everything humorous was very fully developed.

There was little or no restraint imposed upon them. If a dispute arose between any two of the number which could not be amicably settled, they turned off the road, had a set-to, discovered who was the best man, and manfully resumed their march after having afforded no small gratification to a crowd of admiring lookers-on, and settled their dispute to their own satisfaction! There was no officer in charge of the recruits; usually two mounted non-commissioned officers of the troop were told off to keep them together, if possible, a task as difficult as that of Sisyphus—or, which in the language of Hennessy—one of the wildest of the lot—"gave them more nor a dish to wash." The troop always marched a couple of miles ahead of them, and they allowed themselves the liberty of taking a latitude of two miles in addition to that, in order that they might indulge in their pranks and monkey-tricks with the greater impunity.

A damper was destined soon to be thrown on their exhilaration. They arrived in a day or two at Sasseram: this was on a Saturday. The following day, Sunday, being halted, a divine service parade was ordered under a magnificent tope of trees near which they were encamped. During the service several men fell and were carried to the hospital tent; it was imagined that they had fainted—but it was found they were dead! One of those frightful epidemics of cholera (so frequent and so unaccountable in those days) had visited their camp; numbers died during the same night and the following morning. A fatigue party was told off and remained behind to bury the dead, the remainder resuming their march. Many died in the doolies as they were conveyed along the road, and this melancholy state of affairs continued for some days.

Besides this, there were several other memorable incidents on this march which made a deep impression on the writer's mind, and indeed, had no small effect on his body, as well as the other recruits who had the cruel misfortune to be under the protection (?) of the old and trained soldiers who accompanied them. On one particular day the march "was supposed," a favourite expression among the men of the battery, to be a remarkably short one, about three miles, but in which was included the crossing of the Soane, a formidable task for the horses, guns, wagons, &c., &c., there being no bridge, but a ford and the water pretty deep at that. When the bank of the river was reached, the horses were untraced, taken over to the other side by the gunners, and the unfortunate recruits were told off to bring the guns, wagons, &c. across as best they could, being converted into "bastes av burden," as Hennessy avowed, for the purpose, while the old soldiers contemplated the struggles and exertions of the young ones with the utmost composure, and unless compelled by the officers, never affording the slightest assistance, but ridiculing the exertions of the young fellows, which, indeed, were sometimes laughable enough, for the splashing, the tumbling over, the pulling too strong in one place, and not at all in the other, made as ridiculous a spectacle as can well be imagined. Although apparently much put out, Hennessy's anger was mere pretence.

He enjoyed the thing amazingly, and after coolly upsetting a superintending bombardier, he fell prone down himself, and had a good ducking for the sake of his joke.

"See now," said Barney, as the bombardier got up, spluttering and blowing like a military grampus, and disgorging the water he had been condemned to swallow—"he's mixed his liquor; made grog av id ye see, an' he doesn't like the taste! It's not nate enuff for a strong young drinker. Are ye much wet?" he enquired, slyly, while the dripping man stood before him cursing the awkwardness which had apparently caused his fall. "Ye needn't curse, anyhow," said Barney, "ye only had yer share of id, like meself!"

"Bedad," he continued, "we get one consolation out av our misfarten; we'll nayther of as be drownded. Hangin' av coorse, is another matter entirely!"

After infinite labour the task was completed, and the march of three miles assumed the dimensions of thirty—"and Irish miles, too," said Barney. "The divil brake the necks o' them that ordered gintlemins' sons to do such durty work! How do you expect me to be lukin' a commissariat mule in the face, after taken the brid out av his mouth by doin' his work; and no wonder the hoots" (camels) "do be gruntin' at us, whin they see us as bad as thimsilves! Musha now!" he groaned, "what fun people get wid other people's children! Dy'e think I tuk the shillin' in Duke Street, Westminster, to be made a baste av burden? Av that's yer cumpany, John Cumpany, its the worst ivir I was in in me life, an' the sooner I lave id the quicker."

But all their troubles were forgotten when they had a good rest, and the day's labour sweetened their slumbers. They had a halt the next day, and the river being quite close to the camp-ground, a general move of all hands took place in that direction for the enjoyment of a header in the limpid water of the Soane. The day passed pleasantly enough; but as the sun went down their noisy mirth was hushed, and the boldest held his breath, as it was rumoured in camp that two of their comrades, no swimmers, had either unwittingly ventured beyond their depth, or been swept away by the current, and were drowned! A deep gloom overspread the whole party, old and young, and it was increased by every effort proving unavailing to find the bodies.

A fatigue party was left behind on the march of the detachment the following morning—a brother of one of the drowned men forming a unit in the performance of the sorrowful duty—to endeavour to find the bodies and bury them. After long and arduous search the bodies were found in a deep pool, clasped in each others arms. Whether in the agonies of drowning they had grappled with each other in a desperate clutch for life; or whether seeing aid unavailable had chosen that method of ending their brief span, was matter for much conjecture. It was many a day before the incident was forgotten.

They reached Cawnpore in April; the weather was frightfully hot and sultry; the hot winds and Cawnpore devils— eddies of the dust—were blowing furiously; and they the (artillery recruits), were told off to occupy one of the vacant barracks, an agreeable change from canvas. The troops took up their quarters, and the 400 infantry recruits were marched off to the infantry lines. *Khus-khus tatties* (screen mats, made from the roots of an aromatic grass and bamboo), were placed on the doorways of the barracks, which were plentifully sprinkled with water by *coolies* entertained for the purpose, and had the effect of causing the barracks to be tolerably cool during the day. There were no *punkahs* allowed in those days, and at night the men slept outside the barracks in the open, They had not been permitted to enjoy the barracks many days, when the horse and foot artillery recruits were ordered to march and join their respective troops and companies higher up and hero the pay sergeant of the troop to which the horse artillery recruits had been attached, was ordered to pay thorn up and close their accounts. The night prior to that on which they were to resume their march to Meerut, they were summoned to attend the pay-sergeant at his quarters; when there, each recruit was called on to sign his accounts, after having done which, he received *Rs.* 2, with which he appeared to be satisfied.

When the writer was called in and asked to sign, he took the liberty of asking how much money he was to receive after his signature, and told that, as a special case, and out of compliment to his good looks and general appearance, he would receive five *rupees*. To the amazement of the pay-sergeant, the writer declined to sign, for neither his comrade nor himself had received any pay for three months, and had drawn no rum the whole march, while the others had drawn two drams of rum daily. His comrade was then called upon to sign, which he sturdily refused to do, and they were coolly then informed that if they persisted in their refusal, they should be sent to the guard-room—to which abode of bliss they were despatched, after much wrangling, but were released, and again called into the presence, when the writer received *Rs.* 30, and his comrade *Rs.* 20, and then they signed their accounts as having been made up correctly.

This was not the case! The accounts were all wrong, and they were deliberately swindled out of what would have been to them a large sum. The writer got the largest sum because he made the most noise, and showed the most determined front of resistance to the desire that the accounts should be signed; he was perfectly aware that there was a much larger sum due to him, but for the sake of peace and quietness, and knowing full well how hard a matter it would be to obtain redress, he accepted the sum offered him and advised his chum to do the same. When the remaining recruits ascertained how liberally the writer and his comrade had been treated, they fell upon the pay-sergeant *en masse,* and created a great disturbance. They were pacified, however, by the receipt of *Rs.* 3 each in addition to the *Rs.* 2 they had already received on their first signing. They (most of them) spent their money in the canteen that night, and went drunk to their beds in the open air, from which they were roused from their uneasy slumbers in the morning to march to their destination with aching heads and pockets void of coin!

A few volunteers from the troop of horse artillery with which the party had marched from Dum-Dum with a number of horses, were added to their detachment under the command of a young infantry officer. This young gentleman allowed them to march any way, and in any dress—great privileges it must be conceded—provided they struck their tents at sunset and sent them off to the next camp ground, marching themselves at midnight, to enable them to reach camp before sunrise. During the heat of the day they had the tents pitched under wide-spreading umbrageous trees, where they laid on the grass for their beds were intolerable from the hot winds and clouds of dust blowing through the tents. After a few days march the recruits belonging to the foot artillery branched off towards Agra, and they continued their march to Meerut.

The old soldier volunteers rode their horses bare-backed—for no saddles had been transferred with the horses—and the young fellows had to groom them, and lead them to water, but were specially and carefully debarred the privilege of riding them. When they arrived at Haupper, two marches from Meerut, (where the remount stud now is) a tremendous storm burst upon them, blew their tents down, and the floods of rain which descended washed away everything and left them dinner-less! Numbers of large trees to which the tent-ropes had been fastened were blown down, and the whole ground was under water. Here a bold stroke was made by the veterans. They proposed to the young officer in charge to permit the men of the detachment to find their way into Meerut the best way they could ; to allow them two days' rum per man, to be carried in a small cask on a *cooly's* head; the tents and bedding, with the young officer, and a few men to be left in camp to follow on to Meerut when damages were repaired and carriage available. This arrangement was carried into effect; that evening such as wished (so free and easy was their way of doing business), started off for Meerut, and marched all night in the pelting rain.

As for the old soldiers, their chief care was to pay particular attention to themselves, by keeping together, and watching the *cooly* with the cask of grog on his head, until they reached at a small village, where they halted, obtained shelter from the heavy downpour of rain, and set about enjoying themselves after a fashion. In addition to their own, they had a hundred drams of grog with them to enable them to resist the assaults of wind and weather! They (the soldiers) remained snug in quarters enjoying themselves over the purloined grog, while the unfortunate recruits found their way into Meerut about 10 o'clock the following morning, without bite or sup. They were received with a warm welcome from the two troops of horse artillery there stationed, had their wet clothes changed, and a hearty breakfast placed before them, to which they did not fail to do justice, for they had marched twenty miles under heavy monsoon rain, without a morsel of food or grog, and no previous rest for four-and-twenty hours.

After finishing their meal, everyone, save and except the writer and his comrade, were taken to the canteen, treated liberally, and then rested for the day. The old soldiers made their appearance on the following day. The young officer with his small detachment and their rehabilitated camp equipage came two days' later. He mustered the whole, and made them over to the adjutant of the artillery division. This young officer expressed himself to the adjutant as highly satisfied with their conduct during the month or more he had had command of the detachment marching from Cawnpore to Meerut. He had had no trouble whatever with them, he said (except two of the recruits who had been prisoners all the way for theft), and concluded by saying they were a hardy lot of scamps, and that there had been no casualty and no sickness on the march.

They were then told off to the two troops; one-half with the old soldiers and horses, to the new troop (called Geddes'), which was intended to replace the old first troop, first brigade, Horse Artillery (Captain Nicoll's, the present A. C, R. H. A) which had been cut up on the retreat from Cabul, with a few exceptions, *viz.,* Lieutenant Waller, Vincent Eyre (afterwards Sir Vincent), a sergeant and four gunners. The latter four were promoted to be sergeants and ordered never to be reduced.

Of these, three were afterwards invalided home, and two obtained staff appointments in India; one died two years after in Umballa, the other at Dum-Dum several years after. One of these gunners, it may be mentioned here, who had thus been promoted to the rank of sergeant, although a man of great personal courage, was an utter desperado. He was known among his comrades by the sobriquet, of Bullock-horn in consequence of his back and shoulders having been discoloured and hardened by repeated floggings for making away with his regimental necessaries and drunkenness on duty.

After his promotion, on joining his new troop (not to do duty, as he was rendered unfit for service from severe wounds, but waiting the assembly of an invaliding board), the first day he made his appearance in a sergeant's uniform, he "tuk," as he expressed it, "a drop o' stuff, be way av wittin' the sthripes an his arum, an' the goold band an his cap;" and getting speedily into a state of maudlin intoxication, began to cry in a most lachrymose fashion. One of his comrades enquired the cause, and, as well as he could for sobs, the sorrowful man hiccuped out—"Bedad thin, I've had hunders o'stripes an me back, scores o' times, bud I nivir drimt of havin' a palthry three stitched an me useless ould arum! Be gorra its enuff to make a man cry his ould ois out, so it is, fur the maneness o'the thing!" So incorrigible was this man, that previous to his being invalided, he was again tried by a regimental court martial for repeated drunkenness and making away with the gold lace off his cap, and the chevrons off his jacket. The court was at a standstill; it could not punish the delinquent by reduction, but got out of the difficulty by sentencing him to be deprived of the privilege of wearing a sergeant's uniform. The powers of the Court could not reach deprivation of sergeant's pay and pension—that being a special grant by Government to the five men who had escaped the massacre.

The other half (with the two prisoners) was told off to fill up the old (rocket troop) second troop, Second Brigade, Horse Artillery. The two prisoners above mentioned were tried by a court martial some days after and flogged.

They imagined, the writer and his marching comrade, that it was high time for them to set about making themselves comfortable, after a long and tedious march of three-and-a-half-months, and acted accordingly—building castles in the air the while, that, like the conclusion of a fairy tale, "they were going to live happy ever after." Alas, for the vanity of human wishes! A week had barely slipped away in present and anticipated enjoyment, when one fine morning, his highness the adjutant rode up to the barracks, and calling for the writer, his comrade and a third recruit, informed them that their marching was not yet at an end; that they must proceed on to Kurnal, another seven day's march, and by way of getting the matter the sooner over, ordered them to march on the following morning, giving each of them seven days' dry *batta* money—which amounted—the writer loves to be particular—to the immense sum of *Rs.* 1-7-4 per man! A large amount indeed on which to find a fine young man, with a keenly appreciative appetite, for seven days.

Notwithstanding the third of their number having had fever overnight, they started according to order. A tent, a lascar, a camel and its driver—with a copy of the order to march, were all made over to the writer as the oldest soldier, but not the oldest man, for he was but 18 while the others were out of their teens and in the twenties. Misfortune seemed to claim the little party for its own. They had barely advanced a couple of miles on the road, when their third party was rendered completely prostrate by fever. The writer and his comrade held a council of war as to what was to be done under the circumstances, and it was resolved to relieve the camel of his load, mount their sick friend on the beast, and hand him over to the driver. They got a bullock cart and loaded it with the tent and appurtenances, made the baggage over to the lascar, and told him to "*Jao* to Meerut," the writer and his chum proceeding on their journey, and arriving at the end of the first stage, Sirdbana, about fifteen miles, where they rested themselves for the day.

They had a *chatty* (earthen pot) of water boiled, threw a couple of fist-fulls of tea and sugar into it, and indulged in a tall drink of the exciting beverage, They had some cold food in their haversacks which was duly polished off. The same evening they again started, marching all night, leaving the third party to sleep the night out, and take as much rest as he could. On reaching the second stage, it was found that the cold grub being finished, and the inner man requiring to be sustained, they had to arrange a foraging expedition; they got an old hag in charge of the *serai* (resting place for native travellers) to boil water for their tea—they had lots of the latter, and sugar—but nothing else. And it may be as well in this place to hand the name of the writer's comrade down to immortality. His name was Thomas Foster, a Lancashire hawbuck, commonly called Tummy lad—in return for which he good-naturally called every one—whether he knew his proper cognomen or no—Hai lad!

Then Tummy lad and the writer asked the old woman before mentioned to cook them a dish of fowl-curry and rice. Agreeing to do so she began boiling the rice as a preliminary measure, while the pair of interesting youths started for a stroll round the village to look for a fowl. On their way Tummy lad espied one of gigantic proportions, stately and well-fed; upon which he armed himself with a stone, and incontinently knocked the bird over, exclaiming Hai lad! The fowl's throat was soon cut, as Tummy said "to save it from diein," denuded of its feathers, and made over to the old woman as the most substantial component part of their awaited meal.

Towards evening their feverish third party arrived, "dragging his slow length along," and the three sat down to their sumptuous repast, for which, indeed, they had to thank Tummy lad, for was not the corner-stone of the entertainment the trophy, if not of his bow and spear, at all events of his stone? The writer verily believes that since the days of David there never was such a shot with a stone as Tummy lad, and on that short march many a bird fell a victim to his unerring aim. He drily remarked that "they made foine pot-yarbs!" as indeed they did.

They had now reached their last stage before arriving at Kurnal—having made four marches instead of seven in the hottest season of the year. But they were used up, or as Tummy lad phrased it— "dead beat," so they rolled into another *serai*—there was one in every considerable village—and throwing themselves down under a large tree with empty stomachs, and nothing to put into them, for their marching money had run out, they endeavoured to divert the hunger off themselves by having forty winks, trusting to the chapter of accidents and Tummy lad's skill, to get a meal somehow. During their troublous snooze, a gentleman travelling horse-*dak* rode into the *serai* to change his horse, and they awoke to find him making enquiries about them. They jumped up, saluted him *à la militaire,* and he proceeded to question them as to their position: and prospects, and more especially "how the devil they happened to be there, eh?"

They explained to him that they were on their way to Kurnal to join the second troop, First Brigade, Horse Artillery.

He said—"my lads, you have further to go than Kurnal, for the troop has marched on to Ludianah; and you must not stay here tonight—if you do, you stand a chance of waking up in the morning, and finding yourselves without heads!"

They asked him was Ludhiana anyway near Cabul? (as if they dreaded being massacred), but he smiled at their ignorance, and recommended them to procure a bullock cart and make the best of their way into Kurnal at once, the distance being only ten or twelve miles. And here the writer was very forcibly reminded of a saying always in the mouth of one of his old Dum-Dum comrades— "Musha now," said he, when there was any talk of an impossibility being achieved—"its very hard to whistle without the upper lip," and they told the gentleman (whose name they never knew, and whom they never saw again), that they hid neither money nor marbles, and that they couldn't raise the price of the very lightest of refreshments, much less pay for the hire of a bullock cart!

"Ah! well," said their interlocutor, "we'll soon change all that for you—and I suppose you all smoke. Here's some cheroots for you to take the taste of the pipe out of yer mouths;" and he handed them some bundles of magnificent No. 1 Manilas, gave them ten *rupees*, mounted a fresh horse, and; was gone "like a dream in the night!" The writer believes that until he was made acquainted with their story he believed the party were deserters. On enquiry it was found that no bullock cart was available in the village, but they could hire ponies, which delighted them much, as they thought how imposing their entry into Kurnal would be, *à cheval*, even if the ponies were of the smallest.

These ponies however could not be procured till morning, so the party were fain to remain where they were for the night, under the trees, and take their chance of getting up in the morning without their heads. They opened their beds for the first time during the march from Meerut, took out their best jackets, overalls, and boots and spurs, and set about furbishing them up, intending to make a great demonstration, and strike awe and wonder into all beholders on making their equestrian entry into their place of destination. After having completed their self-allotted task they fell fast asleep—having previously had what is technically called a feed of milk, *poorees*, and *chappaties* which cost them one *rupee*—and *Rs.* 9 for hire of the three ponies, about—as was afterwards discovered, when it was too late—twice as much as they should have paid. This is a wicked world my masters! See these innocent youths were imposed on!

Daybreak in the morning brought the ponies and their owners, warning them to "boot and saddle." They fastened up their bedding and other belongings, loaded the camel, and made the animal over to the other and much lesser animal, the driver. Then the word was given to mount; they mounted, but had to hold on "werry tight" by the top-ropes (which it was fervently hoped were strong), one and all being ignorant of the science of equitation.

They eventually reached the old town of Kurnal, and in passing it met an Old Fog (a cant name given to a foot artilleryman, the derivation of which is involved in a deep and awful mystery); he was coming out of a *sooreekhana*—not to put too fine a point upon it—a native grog shop, where he had evidently been solacing himself to advantage. The party accosted him familiarly by the name of Old Fog, and civilly enquired if he would be good enough to indicate the way to the horse artillery barracks.

To which, the Fog replied (highly irate it would appear)— "folly yer nose, ye durty recroots!" So they rode on at a steady walk, (by reason they were afraid of falling off if they increased their pace!), and which pace was considered, besides, to be more stately, and left more time for admiration.

On arriving at the horse artillery barracks, a young damsel, speeding on some domestic errand, happened to pass the party, showing a glimpse of a very natty foot and leg (ladies' dresses being worn short in those days) which excited the admiration of Tummy lad, who exclaimed, loud enough for the girl to hear him.—"Hie lad! si thee! Twig that ere wench's pretty foot and ancle! Hie lad?" He had to be silenced for his rudeness, which brought a deep blush to the girl's cheek, but the blush would have been deeper had she known that two years and a half after she would be the wife of the writer!

They dismounted their ponies, making them over to their owners (who had respectfully attended them, even unto the gates—whether from a doubt of their honesty, or with that lingering desire for *bucksheesh* so dear to the native mind, it is needless now to enquire), dismissed them with a blessing—which, indeed, was all they had to give them—and joined their troop on the 14th of May 1842, after a tedious and protracted march of nearly four months during the hottest season of the year, and that without a taste of the stimulant in so common use—(the writer speaks of Tummy lad and himself). It it bootless to say they wore made much of by the old soldiers—young or old; a fresh arrival in India is always that—by the production of the inevitable grog bottle, and he is sorry to note that in a very short time Tummy and the third party were, as the Irishman said, "complately over-tuk wid tho dhrink!" as were also some of the old soldiers. They tried their best to prevail upon the writer to "take the laste taste in life; jist to cover the bottom of the glass, now," but without effect, as up to that time (and as has been said, although he was a young man, he was an "ould sojer"), he had never tasted spirituous liquor. He found his way to a cot and dreamily dozed until the dinner-trumpet sounded, when he rose like a giant refreshed, and did full justice to the ample meal provided for all hands.

So far as comradeship was concerned Tummy lad and himself were parted on the following day, he being told off to No. 2, and the writer to No. 5 sub-divisions. They took leave of each other with much effusion, for if they were rough they were sincere, and on the principle of "soft words buttering no parsnips," perhaps they might have done as much service to each other as if they had pumped out half the sentimentality expanded over a three volume novel. A dry old soldier, who stood looking on at the *adieus* they were exchanging (Tummy lad was only to be separated from his late chum by a bungalow or two—but then, you see, they were young and foolish), appeared to be highly amused at the scene, and called the attention of some of the men who were busy cleaning their traps, to the unwanted display of feeling: "Wait," he ejaculated, with a sniff, "till the ruff edge is tuk off them!"

"And," he continued, eyeing them with some disdain, "did any of yez hear of what the rat said, when he left his tail in a trap? Ye didn't? Well, says he—that's the rat I mane,—contemplatin' the stump that was left, wid some pity in his oi; well sis he—'the bist av friends must part'—and he said no more. There's nayther av yez losin' a tail," he continued, "an ye might strive an' put up wid the partin' as manfully as the rat did, who had lost a dale more than ayther of yez ivir had!" at which there was a good deal of laughing in which they could not help joining, and so they parted.

CHAPTER 3.

Soldiering

And now, like a young bear, the writer had all his sorrows before him: riding school, drills of all kinds, morning, noon and afternoon; and at night—every night—till a late hour, there were dances arranged for the exercise and amusement of both sexes. For be it known to all men, that at the time the writer speaks of, the station of Kurnal was literally swarming with specimens of the gentler sex; there were widows; there were spinsters, staid and frisky, of a certain or uncertain age; there were blooming damsels, the well-grown daughters of men either of troops or batteries, or other regiments, cavalry and infantry, the various depôts, of which were quartered in the station, their head- quarters being at Cabul, *viz.,*—H. M.'s 44th Foot, and first troop, first Brigade, Horse Artillery (both massacred on their retreat from Cabul); the third troop, first Brigade, Horse Artillery, and 3rd Light Dragoons with General Pollock's force; and the 13th Light Infantry with General Sale at Jellalabad—

And "the nateral, consiquins is," an old soldier explained to the writer, "that thim that knows their husband is did, want to get others; then, again, thim grass widdys isn't partiklar; thim anshint ould maids is av the wan opinyin with thim; an as for the young craters, why, av coorse, they want to sail in the same boat! Begorra Kurnal's a grate place now for a tindir harted yuth like me"—he was as grey as a badger—had lost all his teeth, and was fifty if he was a day—"to come to! I wish," said the old Don Juan, "I was out av id! Here's a widdy now, wid a rowlin' oi, an' sayin' out av the corner av id, as plain as oi can spake, du ye want a faymale partner, sur?

"Thin, agin, thim ould wans that has run the gauntlet av about tin cavalry, an' twenty infantry ridgimints, and who knows how many troops an' batteries, an' sorra husban' they got yet, want to come in at the heel o' the hunt—an' for all their simperin', an' stanoffishness, bedad they'd lep at a chance, like a rooster at a gooseberry, see if they wudn't! Thin, thim young craters, ye see thims only *gulpins* (recruits), and they're losin' their harts half a dozen times a day, thinkin' they'll plaze their eye no matter what follys, an' av they don't make haste an' choose some dacent young fellow,—there's plenty about—they'll be shoved among the old stagers, and then their chance is gone."

So there was dancing and singing in Kurnal; there was marrying and giving in marriage, and the writer contrived to get through his drills, be dismissed from them all, and become a *bonâ fide* duty-soldier in about six months.

In November his troop was ordered to march to Ferozepore to join the army of observation with Lord Ellenborough, governor-general, and Sir Jasper Nicolls, commander-in-chief, to welcome Sir George Pollock and his army from Cabul. A large triumphal arch was erected on the banks of the Sutlej, and the army of observation formed a street for Sir George Pollock's army to pass through, the bands playing *God save the Queen*, colours flying, with cheers and counter-cheers from both armies.

The spectacle was a splendid one, of course essentially military, and the writer believes was the greatest concentration of troops in point of numbers ever got together in India. After the reception, all moved off to their respective camps; the plain of Ferozepore, and even fields under cultivation were covered with tents as far as the eye could reach, forming a scene of apparent confusion, but, in reality, formed on the strictest mathematical principles. There was length, breadth, and depth; the headquarter camp was in the centre; artillery and cavalry on both flanks and infantry divided in the centre, all gravitating inwards towards the great focus, the high civic and military dignitaries.

"I wish," said Dan Brennan of ours, who believed laying out a camp to be a species of conjuring, "I wish some av thim scientifik blokes wud conjure an owld commissariat bullock or two up here in the night. Here we are, bedad, about three months now, 'aten goat's flesh as av we wer Wilshmin, bekase, to plaze the Sicks, the sorra bullock they'll kilt!" which was the case. No bullocks were allowed to be slaughtered, and the force had nothing but goat's flesh, alternated with indifferent and very dubious mutton, for three months.

We very soon got tired of it—but it was "Hobson's choice" with us. Yet, if, as Dan O'Connell boasted, "a coach and six could be driven through any Act of Parliament," there was a way among a certain class, of getting, better; indeed, whatsoever kind of food they wished. The price of grog, after undergoing various fluctuations, had risen from four to eight annas per dram ; those who did not care for the stimulant, took advantage of the "fancy price put on the article," sold it to those who did care for it, and in this way obtained the means of procuring better food. And to a better use the money obtained in this way could scarcely have been put.

Our time was passed in field manoeuvres; outlying picquets, guard mounting, &c, &c. The Sikhs had a large army a few miles off, and they also repeatedly gave us specimens of their field evolutions, which were very grand. The soldiery passed and repassed our camp on their way to and from the town and bazaars of Ferozepore, buying up all the brandy available. It was no uncommon sight for us to see many of them each carrying his bottle—or two—the corks drawn, drinking freely from the bottles as they passed our tents, by the way, we supposed, of acquainting us with the important fact that they could take as good a swig, aye, or even empty a bottle, as here and there a Briton, "av he was from Tipperary itself!"

A tremendous storm broke over the plain, at least, over all the ground on which our camp was pitched, on the night of the 31st December. It was a scene never to be forgotten, the like of which the writer never saw before, and which he fervently hopes he may never see again. The whole plain was under water nearly knee-deep; the most of the tents were blown down; the horses broke loose and, terrified and terrifying, galloped headlong through the camp, and the utmost consternation and confusion prevailed until morning dawned.

During the storm (it was pitch dark when it broke, and the darkness kept, if possible, increasing) not a glimmer of light was to be seen, everyone standing fast, afraid to move and wondering "What next!" The writer was on the quarter-guard, and by dint of great exertion the guard-tent was kept standing. A remarkable circumstance occurred here, which might be only a coincidence) but which wag, among the more superstitious amongst the men, set down as an intervention of Providence. It was this: at midnight, the sergeant of the guard called to the sentry outside to strike 12 on the ghurry, or gong, which, supported on a tripod, (and a mallet being provided to strike it with), finds a place outside all guard-tents. The sentry obeyed the order, struck 12, and then commencing ringing rung without ceasing for a whole hour, and then struck one. When he was relieved (he was a hard-headed old Scotchman) the following colloquy took place between the sergeant of the guard and he:—

"What the divil did ye mane, Sandy, be keepin' up that tamasha on the ghurry fur a whole hour. I wonder ye didn't get tired av id!"

"Weel, sarjint," said Sandy, "I'll joost tell ye what I was daen. We hae a hamely fashon in oor kintraside, o' ringin the auld year oot an' the new year in. Its a fine auld fashon, and blow high, blow low, its aye keepit up. Aud losh man! if we keep it up at hame, whaur were kin' o' Christens, what for no

OFFICERS IN THE BENGAL HORSE ARTILLERY

Bengal Horse Artillery

OFFICER BENGAL HORSE ARTILLERY

Officers of the Bengal Army

in a kin o' hay then place like this, whaur we have Sheeva, an' Deeva, an' Mamet, an sic trash! That's what I was daen I, was ringin' the old yeer oot and ringin' the new yin in! *An'* ye'll see the storm it'll soon blaw oower, noo!"

Whether Sandy was inspired or not this deponent sayeth not but the storm gradually lessened, and what is more, brought magnificent weather with its lessening, for there was no more rain during our stay in camp.

The army broke up about the end of February 1843, and the writer's troop marched back to its old station Kurnal, and he chronicles here the pleasure he felt in experiencing the delight of being carried on the march instead of having to tramp it, as in the days of his youth—for he was, what with his experience of camp life, and "faymale blandishments," beginning to feel very old indeed, altho' he wasn't twenty, and a razor, even in those days of close shavin' was to him a superfluity! The troop reached its quarters at the end of March, and it was a touching sight to witness the devotion with which the fair sex, herein-before mentioned (and glorified) turned out to meet us!

Married, widdyed, grass-widdys, staid damsels, and young and blooming maidens, being duly advertised of our advent, got up what might be supposed to be a full dress parade on their own account, and came a mile or so on the road to meet us, to show the extent of their appreciation of the stalwart warriors, and to air their good looks and becoming dresses at the same time. Their enthusiasm was boundless; and warm as was the greeting on the road, the fervour was much enhanced by the time the horses and guns were secured.

Many a fine young fellow (not to speak of the middle-aged and more expayrinced, was caught in webs matrimonial, woven by some one or other of the deft hands belonging to the sex before mentioned, and, "see me now," the writer's ancient mentor observed—"mark my words, in less nor a couple of months—I'll give them that time to be hookin' their fish —the divil recave the marrigible man jack will be left single round the horse artillery lines!" Whether it was his advice that deterred the writer, or a predisposition to enjoy the life of a bachelor a little longer preponderated, it is not in his modesty to say. He was eligible enough, he was big enough, (6 foot and an inch in his stocking feet an' built conformable;) he had a great capacity for enjoyment, as most healthy well-disposed young people have, and although many allurements were thrown around him; and the former routine of barrack-room life, with the dancing (drinking he still eschewed) in full swing, he stoutly resisted its influence and roamed in *bachelor* meditation, fancy free, "More's the pity!" said a father, with a pair of marriageable daughters on hand, to be disposed of chape! "that a fine young fellow like that, wid the ball at his fut, dosen't give it a kick an' send it into the *padgeree* (the married quarters,) on the hop!"

After a few months a fever epidemic broke out over the station. Kurnal was always a most healthy station, and was known among the troops of all arms, Natives as well as Europeans as the sanitarium of Upper India, until then. The hospitals were over flowing with sick, most of the barracks were converted into hospitals, and the epidemic was attended with such grave results (no joke is intended,) that it eventuated in the condemnation of the station of Kurnal as a military post, at a loss of life which, numerically, would make modern statisticians stare, and about October 1843 the entire body of troops there stationed marched to Umballa, which was destined to be the site of a new cantonment. It was not then a military station, and the troops remained under canvas until June 1844, while temporary barracks were erected for their accommodation. The married people were accommodated (?) in stables, and the horses picketed on the common for a year or two.

After the rains the troops encamped again to enable the Department Public Works, to finish the barracks in course of being built. The annual practice of the artillery commenced; in December, and continued all that month, and the ensuing one of January 1845. Looking at that year, and the subsequent years of his service, the writer finds '45 the most conspicuous, if he excepts the year '57, when on the dreadful 10th of May, on a beautiful Sunday evening, the mutiny broke out at Meerut. It ('45) began pleasantly enough by his marriage at the early age of 21—he was caught in the toils, too, it will be seen, for, as his ancient comrade told him in confidence, and as if it were a fact but just discovered, "the pitcher which goeth often to the well, getteth broken at last"—to the identical young damsel on whose natty foot and ankle Tummy lad had passed the complimentary remark on the day he joined his troop, a circumstance which she remembered perfectly well.

Shortly after this the writer mounted the first step on the ladder of promotion by assuming the chevron of a full blown bombardier; followed shortly afterwards by his elevation to the rank of corporal and pay-sergeant. Lucky fellow, he considered himself, and a "great deal too lucky," some "good-natured friends" (as Sheridan called his detractors) thought him. However that may be, it is not to be wondered at that a habit of taking up the right arm (amounting almost to dislocation), that the chevrons distinguishing his rank might be the more easily admired, had nearly produced more serious consequences as the medical officer in charge of the troop assured him that if he kept squinting in that direction, he must be operated on for strabismus! But youth, and youthful vanity, must plead his best excuses, if any be required.

Unhappily, the state of affairs did not last. It was much too pleasant for that, and a gloom was spread over the station by the reappearance of a cholera epidemic which, even at this day, with all the sanitary improvements which have been discovered and effected, sometimes devastate the stations of Northern India. This scourge swept away many of our comrades; the writer himself was one of the number attacked, and one of the *very* few who recovered. The mortality was so great, that coffins could not be provided for the dead, many of whom had to be buried in their quilts.

When the epidemic had subsided, in October, a new and distinguished commanding officer, joined the troop, in the person of Major Elliot D'Arcy Todd, K.L.S., who had lately been Political Agent in Herat, and whose bravery and talent were widely known in all military circles. His services, and a brief sketch of his life are given' in the appendices, where also will be found a record of the services of the writer.

In January 1944 a most important order was received by the Bengal Horse Artillery. In those days no moustache was worn by the men of the British army saving the dragoons and lancers, and the 3rd Light Dragoons and 16th Lancers being the only dragoon regiments on this side of India at the time, their hirsute facial appendages and embellishments were the envy of the men and the distraction of the women of the service. The order alluded to was that the horse artillery should follow suit in the way of moustache wearing!

Great was the rejoicing; razors were consigned to oblivion; the prices of Rowland's Macassar; all kinds of abominations, known under the generic title of hair oil. The real genuine bear's grease (straight from Russia in twenty ships!) and Universal Hair Grower and Restorer, reached fabulous amounts; and yet the demand exceeded the supply! Old hands were plastering their bristles to soften them, daily, and young fellows were breaking their looking glasses by looking hard at them twenty times a day to see "'av more hair had grown since mornin'." The ladies condemned the movement, since it had enhanced the price of articles more particularly in the province of their toilette, but the wearers were envied all the same!

To give the reader a general idea of the old *melange* of the men of which the troop to which the writer belonged was composed, he has calculated that six-eighths of the number were natives of the land which the poet boasted as being:—

Great glorious and free!

First flower of the earth and first gem of the sea!

One-eighth English, and one-eighth Scotch. The two latter nationalities are easily disposed of so far as regards peculiarities (in an up and down scuffle there might be more difficulty.) The former were regarded by the majority of the troop as quiet, good-natured fellows, and favoured by the cognomen of duff-eaters. The latter were stand-off-the-grass fellows, and awfully clannish, with a gift, however, of takin' guid care o' themselves.

But the Irish! Who shall describe the Protean nature of their phases of character. They "were everything by turns, and nothing long." The first in mischief, merriment, and devilment of all descriptions; brave to temerity, never at a loss for an answer or an excuse, no matter how difficult, the question, or how grave the subject to be discussed. With a "half-laugh, whole earnest" expression of countenance, backed by speech of a similar description; invariably respectful, and perpetually jolly. as Mark Tapley had it, they certainly ruled the roost in the troop. Nor did they abuse the power they possessed; but if a comrade of another nationality got his back up, and ran counter to their wishes, or their line of action, they quietly made their power felt, and the malcontent was fain to do as the rest did, and grin and bear it.

Proud of their descent—if you believed some of them, they were descended from such remote ancestors as Brian Born or Fin Macoul, "or wan av the Sazars, anyhow!" In joke they dubbed themselves Gentlemen, and whatever name or designation they most affected, that they were known by, and it stuck to them even after death! For instance, there was Charles O'Dwyer, one of the most powerful men who ever came to India, and he called himself "a Connaught gentleman"—he belonged to Connaught—and other people called him so too. He had another peculiarity; he was sponge-man to No. 1 subdivision, of the 1st troop, 1st Brigade, Bengal Horse Artillery. No. 1 was the right gun of the troop, and when he had occasion to sign any letter or other document, he invariably affixed to his signature, as his designation, "Sponge-man to the rigid gun of India!"

He was killed in Wheeler's entrenchment at Cawnpore, during the mutiny, while he was fetching water from a well for the women and children, under a heavy fire. Charles O'Dwyer was a particular favourite of Mad Jack, or Hell-fire Jack, as the present General Olpherts was called when he was Captain (the General is a Connaught man too), and it is to be hoped he will not be offended at having his name mentioned in connection with one of the bravest men who ever drew a sword or fired a gun in any service in the world!

Then there was Edward Rowland O'Shaughnessy, a nephew of Sir W. B. O'Shaughnessy. the late director-general of telegraphs. He called himself, and his title was adopted, the pride of Bengal and the terror of India. Many years, after he was invalided home he wrote out to the troop, adding the old and well-known designation to his signature. And here the writer will be pardoned for introducing a story told of the late Terence O'Shaughnessy, son to the Sir William already mentioned, and, of course, a cousin of the pride of Bengal and the terror of India. He was a trooper in the Bengal yeomanry cavalry, and coming home to his tent one night, the regiment being encamped on the maidan, at Calcutta, he stumbled over the adjutant's tent-ropes, and had some difficulty in recovering and sustaining his equilibrium. This gentleman had risen from the ranks (the adjutant is meant) and had just been transferred from a dragoon corps to keep the somewhat unruly spirits of the yeomanry in order, and not being used to their free-and-easy ways, he rushed from his tent, and addressed Terence in no measured terms, concluding with the question: "Who the devil are you, Sir?"

"Ah!" said Terence—"that's it! (hic) that's it! (hic) thought you didn't know me! why! (hic, hic.) everyone knows me. The question (hic) to be solved is (hic) who the h— are you, eh? Dammit can't you (hic) speak?"

Rage prevented the adjutant from articulating, but eventually he stammered—

"Me Sir! By God, I'll let you know who I am. I—am—the—adjutant! Will that satisfy you?"

To which O'Shaughnessy replied with drunken gravity, "Divil a bit! Adjutant!" Here he gave a long low whistle, as if astonished at the disclosure of the rank of the offended officer—and then he drew himself as neatly as possible up to the first position, and contrived to stutter—"Adjutant, eh? Why (hic) I've seen a much better (hic) adjutant than you, standing (hic) on one leg on the ball at the gate of Govern—(hic) Government House!" This filled the measure of the adjutant's indignation, but O'Shaughnessy's punishment was only a night in the guard-tent. Before ending the story of the two O'Shaughnessys, the writer will add a short story about his friend, the pride of Bengal and the terror of India—my old friend Gunner E. R. O'Shaughnessy, who took part in the First Burmese war in 1824-25.

During the war, there being a scarcity of medical subordinates to attend the wounded and sick, my friend was appointed apothecary (temporarily during the war) to the hospital of his own corps, he having followed the medical profession prior to his enlistment into the Bengal Artillery. After the return of the troops from Burmah to their several stations, my friend was promoted to the rank of school-master-sergeant to a brigade of horse artillery, when he became so addicted to the bottle, that he was reduced by court martial to the rank and pay of a gunner.

During his service he was several times helped up the ladder, but unfortunately he could not remain up any time without tumbling down with a great crash; it appeared that the post of gunner suited my friend best, there being no further reduction from that post. He went from bad to worse, and was never off the defaulters' list. On one occasion he was brought before the commanding officer, Colonel G. Brookes (Bully Brookes, as we called him) for being drunk; he was sentenced to drill, and liquor stopped for ever and a day. Not many days after, my friend was brought up again for the same crime, which appears to have brought the colonel to a stand-still as to what sentence to pass on the prisoner. At last he sentenced him to have his rations stopped, which was quite illegal; this sentence was carried out only for a few days, when the colonel thought better of it, and, withdrew the sentence; in the meanwhile my friend had full and plenty from his comrades, for all respected him for his venerable appearance and medical science; when sober he made use of the latter, and kept many of his comrades from hospital by physicking them in barracks.

About this time the order for trying men for habitual drunkenness—(four times drunk in a year) came into force; my friend was about one of the first to be tried by a regimental court martial for habitual drunkenness, and was sentenced to 42 days' imprisonment; about the same time three others were tried for the same offence and were sentenced to receive 100 lashes each, and the commanding officer ordered the court martial on Gunner O'Shaughnessy to reassemble to revise the sentence of 42 days' imprisonment to the lash.

The court must have taken into consideration the man's venerable appearance and his long service of 23 years, so they adhered to their former sentence and my friend escaped the lash. A parade was ordered to see the corporal punishment carried out, the proceedings of each court martial was read out and the three men were flogged; while all felt for them, Gunner O'Shaughnessy's court martial and sentence was also read out, and the commanding officer appeared quite displeased at the court not revising the sentence; he released the prisoner with disgust, to the joy of all on parade, except the colonel himself.

This act of displeasure shown on the part of the commanding officer, and the act of justice and leniency of the court, was a warning to my friend; a few months after he was invalided and sent back to Old Ireland, (from whence he came) on a pension of one shilling per day. He left off his drinking propensities after getting home, walked in respectable society once more, married the lady—to whom he paid his addresses prior to enlisting, was appointed Governor to the Galway Union and on meeting an old troop-mate one fine day in Ireland he made over his shilling a day pension to him for old acquaintance sake.

I have already stated in another part of my narrative when, the old veteran wrote out to his old troop.

The writer cannot refrain here from saying a few words in favour of his old commanding officer Colonel Brookes; it was generally admitted that he was severe and eccentric in weighing off prisoners, for he had scores brought before him almost daily; having under his command three troops of horse artillery and two light field batteries, (he had a great variety of men to deal with) at the same time he was *very* forgiving, but in a bullying manner; for instance whenever he took the whole brigade out for a field day (about twice a week) and the manoeuvring was executed to his satisfaction he would dismiss the brigade, by ordering his trumpet-major to sound the flourish, which meant the captains were to take their respective troops and batteries home, and he followed after.

While the horses were being rubbed down he paraded himself up and down the horse lines until the horses were dry and cleaned, he then ordered his trumpet-major to sound dismiss: now comes the time for all defaulters of each troop to step out to their respective captains with a request to see the colonel, their request is granted, they are marched up each captain taking his squad before the colonel, who puts the question, "what do all these men want?"

Each captain replies, "they wish to see you, sir"—The colonel asks each man "Well what do you want?" Each man has the same request to make, to have their sentence forgiven, some promise him to keep out of trouble for one month, others for two, others for six and so on; he gives them a bullying and ends with saying, "now, if any of you vagabonds are brought before me within three months I will double your sentence, now go to your barracks and begin a new leaf." But any morning the manoeuvring displeased him, he rode off home without dismounting at the horse lines. He always rode from two to three horses at his field days, to keep them in good trim, he being a crack horse-man. He was like a second father to me for he several times gave me a telling off, at the same time promoting me step by step when promotion was least expected.

Then, again, we had Bruff Brennan, who was called and rightly so, the ugliest man in the troop and he had worn the belt which distinguished him as such for fourteen years. But he was not content with his designation, and every yearly draught of recruits which joined the troop was rigidly scrutinised by Bruff, and individually subjected to a close examination for the purpose of discovering whether there was among the number an uglier man than himself. At last after weary waiting, one fine day, a strong draft joined, and Bruff, being "three sheets in the wind"—he was seldom otherwise, poor fellow—proceeding on his usual tour of inspection, stumbled on a young fellow who really far exceeded him in facile exterior. He had no bridge to his nose, to speak of; he squinted; one cheekbone was higher than the other, and he had asinine ears, pendant on his shoulders, "Bedad," said Bruff, "you'll do!"

He waited till the recruits were told off to the different sub-divisions, and then requested the staff sergeant, as a great favour, to post that young man to his sub-division. "Give me his name sir," said Bruff, "'av ye plase, an' be gorra, I'll make a man iv him!"

The request was granted, and old Bruff walked up to the young man, tapped him on the shoulder, and saying— "lave it there!" held out his hand to be shaken—which was done. Bruff continued— "Me dacent boy, I'm gain' to make this belt over to you! (handing a belt to him.) I have carried it for the last 14 years for being the ugliest man in the throop, but, now that I have found one that bangs Banagher for looks (and Banagher banged the divil), aye, faith, even Barber Pike, who ate his way out of a warehouse av tripe widout a grain of salt, you're the man to wear it! An I hope ye'll live to wear it as long as I have! But you mustn't take it over dry; divil a, fut; we must wet id. I have a bottle av the rale stuff itself—we'll crack that, an' christen you Beauty! Call your friends to join us, for this is a holiday on account av you youngsters joinin'."

The proposed jollification came off but Beauty did not wear the belt so long as old Bruff. He died 12 years after he received it, from blood-poisoning, after dissecting a diseased horse. A few days before his death he was following the commanding officer Major Tombs, through the horse-lines, when suddenly the chief turned on him and snapped out— "Farrier Hyde, did you ever grin through a horse collar?"

"No, sir," was the reply.

"Hem!" said the major, walking on thoughtfully—"if you had, you know, you'd have won, sir! You'd have won!"

Besides Bruff Brennan's peculiarity, he had a speciality which stood him in good stead, and that was, that no horse in the troop could throw him, and he was by far and away the best horseman in it for the first 15 years of his service, after which he gradually broke down from hard work, so that he was invalided and sent home to Ould Ireland after 21 years service, riding in the pole of No. 2 gun the whole time. Whenever an outrageous brute of a horse had to be trained before being put into harness, Bruff was called upon to "witch the troop with noble horsemanship;" at which he used to be delighted, for when once he was in the saddle there was no getting him out of it, until he was ordered to dismount. He lapped his body round the horse from his ankle to his fork, with stirrups or without—it was all the same to Bruff—threw his shoulders well back, and there he sat, as firm as a rock; he was far from being a handsome-looking horseman, but there never was a better sat in pigskin!

Then we had a man whom hundreds (may the writer say

thousands?) of the readers of these lines must remember—Byrne, the Irish poet—the "hero of 132 fights." After he obtained his discharge he resided in Barrackpore in an old hut which he christened Mount Terrible, and used to travel to and fro on the Eastern Bengal Railway, and wander about Calcutta, disposing of his own (and frequently other people's) compositions for a livelihood. He died at Mount Terrible in the old hut, There is a story told of old Byrne that, upon one occasion being tipsy, and he was quarrelsome in his liquor, he had an argument with an old Fog, who was in a similar condition to himself, and getting the best of it, the old Fog lost his temper and knocked Byrne down, dryly observing, when he had gathered himself together, "ye can go home, now, and say ye're the hayro av a hundred an' thirty- three fiyhts, an' I'll nivir kontrdik ye!"

Byrne was a bit of a lawyer, and, like Coriolanus, was fond of haranguing a mob. He would much rather entertain an audience of young fellows, than old hands; they bled more freely, and—for there was a great deal of the Münchhausen about him,—he could throw the hatchet out of sight—handle and all! He used to tell a story, which, if true, said something for his sharpness. When stationed somewhere up-country, (he was a sergeant, at the time) it appears that he was the sergeant of the quarter-guard. He had been drinking before the guard mounted, and there happening to be one of the troop dances on the board that evening, he made over charge of the guard to the corporal and sallied down to the bungalow where the dance was to take place, with his belts on, just as he had mounted guard. He admired the decoration and the arrangements, of course there was the usual sideboard, at which a comrade sergeant presides, who handed a peg to Byrne, who was in the act of drinking it, when the quarter-master sergeant tapped him on the shoulder. Byrne turned round, still holding the glass in his hand, and said: "Pardon me a moment, Sir," finished the contents at a gulp, and "prepared to receive cavalry."

"What are you doing away from your guard, sergeant Byrne?" quoth the staff-sergeant.

"Why, sur," said Byrne, "I kem to see how they were all gettin' on!"

"They ought to be obliged to you," was the answer. "Go back to your guard; the provost will keep order here."

"Very good, sur," said Byrne, making off.

As he journeyed, he met two sergeants of the 60th Rifles bound for the dance, each with a demijohn of rum under his arm. They sat down in the verandah of the padgeree; wrote their name and rank in full in the contents of one, and parted, they to do a little in the way of the light fantastic, and Byrne to join his guard. In doing so, he mistook the guardroom window for the door, and, with a tremendous crash, fell in among the astonished guard. He was, of course, made a prisoner, and a sergeant sent to relieve him.

He was tried by a regimental court martial for being drunk on duty. A district was applied for, but the general officer commanding the division would not grant it, and ordered a regimental, which was lucky for the hayro.

On a court martial, let it be known, that the junior members of the court are sworn by the president, and then the senior of the junior members swear him. Byrne knew this very well, and kept his eye steadfastly fixed on the proceedings. With the exception of the president, the members were all young officers bored by their having to attend the court, and eager to get away to their breakfast, or their room's, or what not, and the proceedings were hurried on. The junior members were sworn, but the president forgot to have himself sworn, and when Byrne was called upon to plead, he cooly declined, saying the court was not properly constituted, and claimed to be released. The president took counsel with the commanding officer, got a wigging, was told that Byrne was right, and the "Hayro of 132 fights," was once more a free man! How he chuckled over that story! "Be gorra, sur," he would say, "that night at mess, the commading officer said, 'I hear so and so (the president) is goin' to publish a new edition of D'Aguilar on court martials, and Byrne is goin to edit it ; he ought to for I think he knows most about it!'"

The order for trying men for habitual drunkenness—four times drunk in a year—or in certain other circumstances detailed in the warrant, was issued in 1844, and was the cause of a vast amount of punishment in the troop. Courts martial were assembled almost daily, and the punishment awarded for these offences was corporal, and never under 100 lashes. And the heart of the writer has often bled for good and brave old soldiers, who had spent the best of their days and shed their blood for their country, suffering this degrading punishment in consequence of their addiction to liquor, fostered and encouraged (or at all events winked at) by the very authorities who were punishing them. Previous to the issue of this order, no soldier belonging to ours was ever tried by court martial for simple drunkenness. Such a thing was never dreamt of, unless the man was drunk under arms, or for theft, or other disgraceful crime. No one felt for a man who was flogged under such circumstances, while all felt for the man who had only been drunk.

The flogging system never put a stop to drunkenness in the old Bengal Artillery, Horse or Foot. On one occasion, at Peshawar, the writer heard Colonel R. H. who was surrounded by a group of officers, old and young, who had been discussing this very question, (for the writer heard them), addressing them thus: "Gentlemen," he said, "all the warrants in the world won't stop drinking with the men." (He took a young gentleman by the arm to emphasize his observation, and directing their attention to the north west, continued) "Do you see that peak?" pointing to a very high one in the Khyber Pass, "place a Bengal Artillery-man alone on the top of that peak in the morning, and he'll be drunk before night, wherever it may come from! Upon my soul," he went on, "I think they could get liquor out of the rock itself!"

Blessed be providence, the writer saw a wonderful change

for the better in the habits of the men before he left the old Bengal Horse Artillery. He saw the crime of drunkenness, and even the habit itself, reduced almost to a minimum in other troops and batteries, and takes credit for having himself assisted in the good work in his own. This wasn't done by punishment! but by the introduction of a reading-room, a coffee-shop, and malt liquor, but not much of the latter. For example, the writer's troop was quartered in Peshawur from 1850 to the end of 1853 and he has often seen the orderly sergeant drawing the troop's rum in a quart bottle! for, say, about four old soldiers, who imagined, foolishly, that the stimulant could not be done without!

In those days there was no draught malt liquor issued to us, but the writer obtained permission from his commanding officer to purchase such quantity of bottled beer and porter as was daily required. This cost *Rs.* 12 a dozen, and was issued to the men at half price, say, eight *annas* per bottle, the difference being accounted for from the canteen fund accumulations. The men had their comfortable bottle of beer or porter and a snug room in which to enjoy it.

The scheme was highly successful for it harmlessly absorbed the spare money the men might be possessed of, for which they received a *per contra* of enjoyment, and Major Waller had a sober, steady troop for the remainder of the writer's time in it.

CHAPTER 4

Moodkee

"Every schoolboy knows," said Lord Macaulay, and we really don't know why we should not say so too, for he was a historian, and we are but little less, that the campaign of the Sutlej was fought in the year 1845-46; and it may be said, without the fear of contradiction by critics (the *Saturday Review* not excepted), that it was at once the most brief and most glorious in the records of any country.

With a comparatively small force, the British army opposed, and that successfully, an invading Sikh army, said to be composed of 60,000 men, with as complete a train of artillery as the time could produce; and utterly routed them in four pitched and desperate encounters—those of Moodkee, Ferozeshah, Aliwal and Sobraon—and that, too, within the space of eight weeks.

Such a result might lead to the conclusion that the force with which we had to contend was a mere rabble. No greater mistake than this could possibly be made, for they were "foemen worthy of our steel." Originally a warlike race "born soldiers and centaurs" as they have been called, well-trained and disciplined by European officers, French it is believed, the Sikh force was no contemptible enemy. Nothing could be more superbly mounted than their cavalry, and their artillery has been described by an able and experienced writer as "second to none." This will amount (prejudice apart) to stating broadly that they were just a shade in rear of the grand Old John Company Bahadoor's Flying Horse Artillery, the corps which the writer of these lines had the honour and pleasure of serving in for twenty-five years, and which were then, and always had been, the real Simon Pure,—the "Second to none itself".

From the foregoing it will be seen that it was no mere child's play we were engaged in. We had to face men who could give and take as lustily as their opponents; and who "proved their position," as the logicians say, in this campaign, in fair stand-up fights, in which, although beaten, they were never conquered. The latter process overtook them in a subsequent campaign, fought three years' after, in 1848-49.

In December 1845, one of the most eventful years of the writer's service, the Sikhs had made up their minds to invade India, and with this object in view they crossed the river Sutlej, in those days our frontier boundary. At this time, the troop to which the writer belonged, was under the command of Major Elliott D'Arcy Todd, Knight of the Persian Order of the Lion and Sun, and was stationed at Umballa. Intelligence reached us there of the hostile movements on the part of the Sikhs on the 8th or 9th of December 1845, and on the 11th we made our first, march towards the scene of action. Two days before we marched, we buried the wife of our commanding officer, a lady universally and deservedly beloved; and regretted.

Shortly after noon of the 18th December we neared the village of Moodkee. We had marched some 20 miles that morning, over heavy ground, without breaking our fast previous to starting, and it may be taken for granted that we were delighted to reach camp, nearly exhausted as we were with hunger, thirst, and toil, and little did we imagine what was to happen before the day was closed. On halting and parking our guns, the first attention was of course, given to the horses; these we groomed and led to water but the water was so foul that thirsty as they must have been after their long and harassing day's march the poor animals refused to drink it. It became time, after that, to think of ourselves, and we resolved ourselves into a committee of the whole troop, the question being should we pitch our tents, or pitch into our breakfast. It is hardly necessary to say that the latter proposition was unanimously adopted. But, notwithstanding all this, neither measure was destined to be carried out.

Whilst seated round the coffee-boiling fire; and waiting with the patience of so many Jobs, a dispute arose between a corporal who had relieved the writer of the charge of the mess on marching, and himself, which resulted in an adjournment outside the camp to settle the matter by a combat *à l'outrance*, or slogging as such encounters were generally called by the men of ours. We had hardly commenced operations, however, when we heard the alarm being sounded. This of course put an end to the little game we intended playing for another of a more serious nature. We immediately made off to our guns leaving our breakfast un-tasted—and, in addition to that, the reader will be pleased to note that there was a tub full of grog, all ready for issue, untouched!

While standing to our guns we saw the governor-general and the commander-in-chief, with the whole staff, galloping towards the camp, preceded by the trumpet major of the 4th Native Lancers, sounding the alarm. Seeing no token of the enemy, however, a party from each gun was detached and sent back to harness and bring up the horses. These were soon put-to, and all was ready: true it was that some of our men were in their shirt-sleeves, but that didn't matter.

Our gallant brigadier-general, Brookes[1] the (Bully Brookes before alluded to) now took us in hand. As a preliminary, he reminded us of the instructions he had often given us in Umballa at his field-movements, which ran something as under:—

"Now, my men, when, at the gallop, if you see me drop the

---

1. This officer joined the service in 1818, and died in London in 1883, after serving no less a period than 75 years in the gallant old corps.

point of my sword, so" (suiting the action to the word) "go as if the divil were after you: when I raise it so" (indicating the motion) "pull up; and when I give the flourish, so" (and here he gave a tremendous one indeed), "come about, and un-limber!"

Taking up his position in front, he gave the word: "Advance in column of troops from the right," and five troops of horse artillery, consisting of 30 guns, moved off at a gallop, followed by two nine-pounder batteries (12 guns) at a more leisurely pace. We had not advanced far when the round shot from the enemy's artillery began rolling and plunging among the horses' legs like so many cricket balls, but were not quite so harmless as they looked, for they broke several of our horses' legs. A hair-brained lieutenant of ours (Wheelright) took a fancy that he might stop one of their balls and return it to them; he made the trial, and had the mortification of having his right arm disabled as the result of his experiment, and he returned to his guns, cursing his ill-luck at being thus disabled before having had an opportunity of using his splendid Damascus blade, which he had just received as a present from his father at home. The major reprimanded him sharply for his language, and ordered him to the rear.

But the writer is anticipating: The work of the afternoon may now be said to have fairly commenced. We were under fire, and a cheer rang out "for the 12 months' *batta*." At about this stage of the proceedings we got the order "Front form line"—"left about"—"prepare for action"—"with round shot load, and blaze away!" It was just then Lieutenant Wheelright met with his accident.

The Sikhs lost no time in paying us back in our own coin—and that with interest, for they could fire three shots to our two by having the powder and shot in one bag.

We sustained many casualties in this purely artillery duel, and there were many narrow escapes. There were some terrible sights to be seen; and the writer saw one in particular which he will never forget. A vents-man of one of our guns was actually running about disembowelled; the powder-pouch worn on his side had been struck by a shell and exploded. Some of the escapes were absolutely miraculous. A corporal had the port-fire in his hand shattered with a round shot while he was in the act of firing his gun, and he had also to be reprimanded for the language he used on the occasion. It may here be added, that this very non-commissioned officer had to be helped in and out of the saddle from weakness, the result of a long and painful illness: he subsequently died from exhaustion.

The present writer had rather a close shave himself on the occasion—the horse he was riding appeared very uneasy about the head, and at the same instant he himself felt a very peculiar sensation in his own right ear, on stooping forward to examine the horse's head he found its right ear split. The rear-rank man had trained this horse, and the writer turned in his saddle to inform him of his favourite's misfortune. The man was leaning over his holsters at the front of the saddle, as if resting himself. On attempting to rouse him, he literally sprang out of the saddle, fell to the ground and rolled over, face uppermost; a ball had passed through the horse's right ear, and passing by the writer's right ear, penetrated his comrade's right eye. Its direction was perfectly straight.

On looking back to our wagon train, the writer saw that another of his comrades had fallen; he too, had been shot through the right eye: looking to his left, he saw a gunner, an old friend of his, sitting up in his saddle after a round shot had passed through his breast; he had to be lifted out of his saddle, put into a *doolie*, and carried to the rear. These sights, were not the most pleasant, and were calculated to make a young soldier rather squeamish than otherwise, but the disagreeable feeling soon wore away.

This desperate game continued to be played for sometime, when the two nine-pounder batteries came up, one on each flank, and we had now 42 guns in full play. These the Sikhs evidently found too many for them, for their fire sensibly

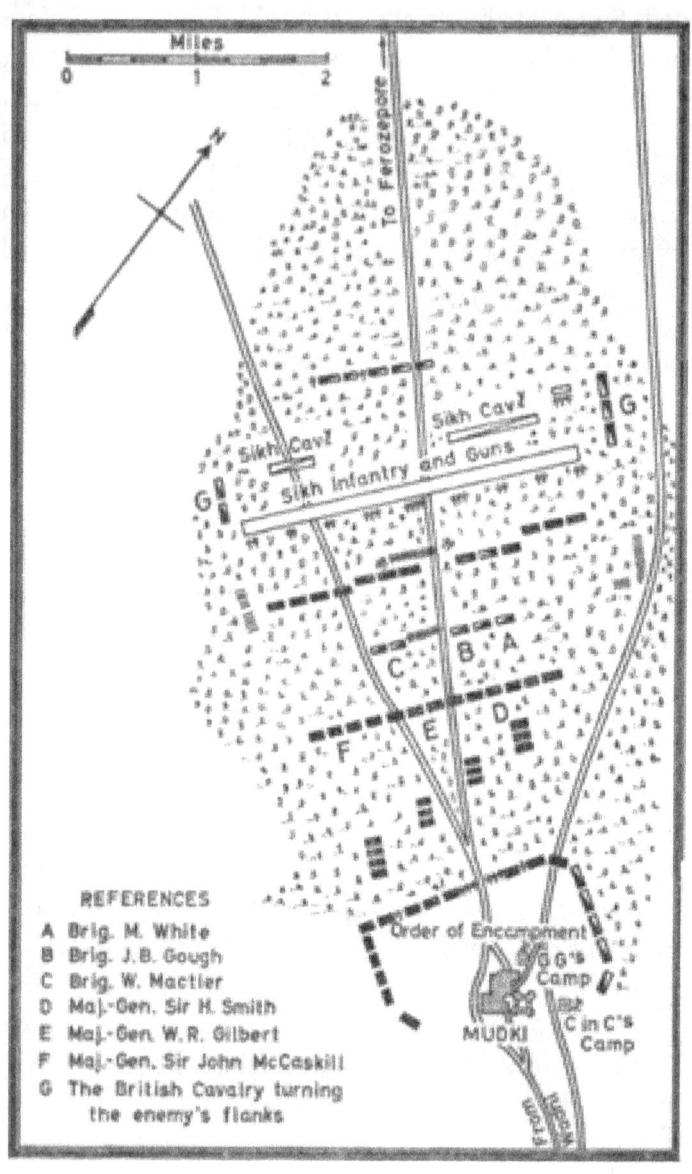

BATTLE OF MUDKI, DECEMBER 18, 1845

slackened, and we received orders to "cease firing," but owing to the excited state of the men, Bully Brookes, our brigadier, found no small difficulty in having his order obeyed; and it must be confessed that a few more rounds were given on our own account, before limbering up. Just then our cavalry came to the front, under Brigadiers Gough and White, and executed some brilliant manoeuvres. They soon put the enemy's cavalry to flight, and silenced their guns, but only for a time.

During the course of the operations just described our infantry had been drawn up immediately in rear of our guns.

We now made our second advance, and soon after found ourselves pretty close to a rather dense jungle of low stunted brush. Here we unlimbered again, and the cannonade was renewed on both sides, with terrible effect. Limbs and heads were carried away in all directions, and in many instances men were literally cut in two. Once more the "ceasefire" sounded. The infantry—some twelve battalions—now passed through the intervals of our guns, and formed line in front. "With ball cartridge, load!" was the order they received, and surely such a ringing of ramrods down the barrels of old Brown Bess, of happy memory, was never heard before at one time. Then they got the order to "shoulder,"—"quick-march," and went out to meet their foe.

Our fighting may now be said to have ceased, and that of the infantry to have commenced. They started with file firing; then volleys by companies; then from regiments; and, finally, from the entire line. On our infantry advancing we followed up steadily till we heard the word of command "Charge" given, at which we stood up in our stirrups and gave the gallant fellows three hearty cheers.

It is of course impossible for the writer to describe the doings of our red coats with any degree of accuracy, not being possessed of the wondrous faculty of Sir Boyle Roche's bird, who could be in two places at once; but as the narrative would be incomplete without such a description, the following extracts are given from an authentic and eloquent account of the battle.

"Under Majors General Sir Harry Smith, Gilbert, and Sir John McCaskill, our infantry now opened fire in echelon of lines on that of the enemy, then almost invisible among the brushwood, the jungle, and the darkness of the approaching night, their exact position being only defined by the red fire of their musketry flashing through the gloom."

"The position of the enemy," says Sir Hugh Gough, in his despatch, "was such as might have been expected from troops who had everything at stake, and who had long vaunted of being irresistible. Their ample and extended line, from their great superiority of numbers, far out-flanked ours, but. this was counterbalanced by the flank movements of our cavalry."

"When the attack of our infantry began, the steady roll of fire they poured into the Sikh lines soon convinced the latter that they had met with a very different race from the tribes of India, and their whole force was gradually driven from position to position with great slaughter, and the loss of seventeen pieces of artillery, some of which were of heavy calibre. Towards the close of the act-ion Sir Robert Sale, to whom Britain and India were so much indebted, had his left thigh shattered by a grape shot as he led on his division, and the wound proved mortal."

"The veteran Sir John MaCaskill received a ball in the chest, and falling from his horse immediately expired. Our infantry invariably resorted to their never-failing weapon, the bayonet, whenever the enemy made a temporary stand, and far over the sandy plain, from time to time, in the dark (for there is no twilight in India) rang the hearty hurrahs of the British, mingling with the strange guttural shouts of the Hindustanees. Night only saved the latter from total destruction, for the battle was continued during an hour and-a-half of dim starlight, amid clouds of whirling and blinding dust from the dry and arid plain, which at times obscured every object."

The strength of our troops engaged consisted of 3,850 Europeans and 8,500 native cavalry and infantry with 42 guns.

Our total loss in killed, wounded and disabled, amounted to 873 of all ranks. The losses of the Sikhs were still greater, as they amounted to thousands, and among their wounded was La Singh, their leader, who narrowly escaped being taken prisoner. His discomfited troops fled to their camp at Ferozeshah while the British returned to their camp at Moodkee about midnight. The whole of the captured guns were destroyed, and left in the fort there. Brigadier Brookes reported that four more guns had been dismounted by the fire of the horse artillery, and left on the field for want of horses to bring them away. On reaching camp the major gave the men great praise for their steadiness; and it was well deserved, for not a man of the troop, except the major and a trumpeter, had been under fire before. It is wonderful, let the writer note, how numerous are the changes which occur in a troop in the course of long service.

Twenty years before the date of this action, the commanding officer had fought with the same troop at Bhurtpore as a subaltern. There was not a man left of the troop who had been there, the last—the hundred and fifteenth casualty—having died a few months before. This was a sergeant of the troop, who had kept a record of the daily distribution. He calculated that the troop, from casualties, deaths, transfers and discharges had been over three times renewed since Bhurtpore. He remarked: "there have been a hundred and fourteen deaths alone." He made the hundred and fifteenth the very next day! Beyond unlimbering the guns nothing was done. The horses remained in harness, and put-to, with their blankets over them, and we threw ourselves, wrapped in our cloaks, on the ground, ready for any emergency. Any one can imagine our condition.

We had marched twenty miles, or more; we had fought and won an engagement, and now had mother earth for a palliasse—and above all, had been rewarded by the consoling reflection that we had not had a mouthful of food or a drink of water since the previous evening!

We had not long been lain down when a noise was heard in front where our infantry was bivouacked; we were up in a moment and at our respective posts—all in the dark. The cause of the alarm was the bringing in of one of the guns of our 3rd troop, under the command of Major G. H. Swinley, which had to be abandoned in the jungle during the engagement owing to the loss of its entire team of horses with their riders; of the latter, four were killed and two disabled.

There was quite a story about one of the two disabled gunners, whose name was Fox; he was an old soldier, having completed his 21 years' service, and was left behind at Umballa on the march of the troop. He never showed up until seen in action, for he had deserted from the depot and followed the troop to the action at Moodkee, where he had his light shoulder shattered by a cannon ball. He was, of course, taken to the hospital, where his arm was amputated, but before undergoing the operation he quietly said to the medical man, "Doctor, dear, just you give me a chaw of baccy, and go ahead!"

Old Fox was to have been tried by a court-martial for desertion, instead of which he was promoted to the full rank of corporal, the corporal of his gun having been killed. He was invalided, but the sturdy old fellow unfortunately died on his way home. Lieutenant Pollock, of the same troop (son of Sir George Pollock, the Cabul hero), was brought in on this gun with his leg shattered. He died the following morning having refused to be operated on. Captain Dashwood, commanding the 1/1 Horse Artillery, had one of his legs shattered also by grape shot, and his horse killed under him as he led his troop: his wound proving mortal; the staff serjeant was killed at the same time; the trumpeter had five grapeshot wounds, all on the right side, from his ankle to his shoulder, his right arm was broken, and his horse shot under him, but it is pleasant to know that the riddled musician survived to enjoy a pension.

No further incident worthy of record occurred during the night, On the 19th, the whole force was again formed upon the plain of Moodkee in battle order. Here a couple of men were sent into camp to bring our breakfast, which we shared with our infantry comrades, who had been told off to cover our guns. In this position we remained all day, smoking our pipes and chatting about our lost comrades who had been left on the field where they fell, and were lying stark and stiff under the rays of a scorching sun without a chance of being buried! During the day all the wounded were brought in; but not all the dead. We returned to camp in the evening, and picketed the horses, returned our guns to the park, and were obliged to remain another bitter cold night without our tents, and, wonderful to say, felt not a whit the worse. Later on in the night we heard a band playing in the camp which helped to cheer us up.

It was the fine band of the governor-general welcoming a fresh addition to the force, in the shape of two heavy guns, escorted by H. M.'s 29th Foot, the 1st Bengal European Light Infantry and two regiments of Native Infantry, the 11th and 41st. And now it was with a chivalrous magnanimity, worthy of Bayard, that the governor-general, Sir Henry Hardinge, who had served throughout the long Peninsular War. offered to serve under Sir Hugh Gough, by whom he was appointed second in command of the army, and, said the general order, "Officers are directed to obey any orders emanating from him," which they were not bound to do, so long as he, although the supreme head of the Government, exercised only a civil authority.

On the 20th, having nothing to do but bury the dead, we pitched our tents. In the evening an order was passed round that we were to move out, with the least possible delay and noise, early the following morning.

Chapter 5

Ferozeshah

At 3 a.m. on the 21st we were under arms, after a hearty breakfast, consisting of coffee, what was popularly called "elephants' lugs" and onions. As the dish is unknown to Soyer, or any other celebrated *chef d'cuisine,* the writer may describe it: "Elephants' lugs" were neither more nor less than huge cakes made from very coarse attah and bran, mixed with chopped straw, for elephants! Each man had one of these issued, to last him for the whole day, no other bread being to be had. We marched off, leaving our tents standing and our bedding tied up.

Our route lay over the field of Moodkee, and on leaving it a mile behind us, we came across a number of bodies of our infantry and cavalry who had fallen on the 18th. They had been stripped of their arms, boots and any valuables they might have had about their persons. These men had evidently advanced too far to the front on the final charge of that day. As a halt was called just then, we set about digging graves for the poor fellows, but were disturbed in our work by the arrival of the commander in-chief, who quietly remarked that "this was no time for such business."

The advance was again sounded, and we had not proceeded far when we fell in with Littler's force, consisting of 5,500 men and 21 guns, which had pushed on from Ferozepore to join the commander-in-chief. We were again halted as the heat was intense, the dust sharp and thick, and water very scanty, but nevertheless, the time passed pleasantly enough, for we were engaged in looking up shipmates (*i. e.*, men who had come to India in the ship) and townies (fellow townsmen), in the force that had joined us. It was in the midst of these recognitions and greetings that we heard the first shot from the enemy, but in an instant every man was in his place, and the different columns moved off to their allotted positions. We were in the left column under Sir Henry Hardinge.

Our route now lay through a dense jungle, and on emerging from which we found ourselves upon a level plain, and exposed to a most murderous artillery fire. Indeed, so hot was it, that an infantry regiment, the 9th Holy Boys, covering our guns, was ordered to lie down, not, however, before wide gaps had been made in their ranks by chain-shot. It is believed their colonel was among the number killed. At this juncture an A.-D.-C. rode up with instructions for the horse artillery to gallop to the front and open fire, which was done. Here the writer's comrade's horse was killed by a cannon shot through the body, which left him with him one leading horse.

The A.-D.-C. who brought the order never returned to his chief. A second A.-D.-C. soon galloped up with orders to approach yet more closely to the enemy's batteries ; this second A.-D.-C. met the same fate as the first, for both their horses were seen running wild about the field without their riders. It being found that our light six-pounder guns produced but slight effect on the enemy's heavier metal, before carrying out the last order, our major, evidently with the object of ascertaining how close it would be necessary for him to advance, laid one of the guns himself, ordering it to be fired ; he stepped aside to note the result, which must have disappointed him, as he was observed to stamp his foot impatiently.

He turned round in search of his horse, and not seeing it, he said—his last words, alas!—"Bancroft, where is my horse?"

Pointing to the direction in which the animal was stand-

THE BRITISH ARMY
as drawn up at the commencement of the
BATTLE OF FEROZESHAH
at 3.30 P.M. on the 21st December, 1845.

Fought under the personal command of H.E. Genl. Sir Hugh Gough Bt. G.C.B. Commander in Chief

H.E. Genl. Sir H. Gough, Bt. G.C.B. Commr. in Chief

Major Genl. Sir J. Littler, K.C.B.

Br. Ashburnham — Br. Reid
2-3pr 34 77 44 62 73 HM44 2 Troops
Batteries H.A.

Br. Harrison
3 Irr. B.L. Cav. 5 Lt Cav. B. gd.

Lieut. Genl. Sir Harry Hardinge, G.C.B.

Brigadier Wallace
Br. Brooke
Troop 2-9 pr
9 Foot 26 29 N.I. HMLI 2N.I. 8 inch Battn. 2 Troops
2N.I. 73N.I. Howitzers H.A.

Major Genl. Gilbert

Br. Macleran — Br. Taylor
1st 29 N.I. 45 41 HM.80 HM.29 1 Troop H.A.

Major Genl. Sir Harry Smith, K.C.B.

Br. Ryan — Br. Hicks
42 48 HM.50 43 26 HM.31
One Troop
H.A.

Br. White
4 L.C. 3 L.D.

ORDER OF BATTLE OF FEROZESHAH

ing, the writer answered: "There he is, Sir!" The words were scarcely uttered, when he saw the gallant major lying at a little distance from his horse—headless! The shot must have struck him full in the face, for there was no trace or vestige of his features to be seen. At the same moment the writer felt a dreadful shock on his right side, and his right arm involuntarily whirled round his head (it was the same cannon shot which killed our major.) He was at the time picking out a quid of tobacco from a comrade's pouch to moisten his lips withal.

Feeling that he was hit, he returned the pouch, with the left hand, remarking—"here, take your pouch, I have lost my arm!" The shot had passed between his body and right arm, carrying away his pouch and belt on the one side, and the soft parts of the arm itself on the other. Being disabled, he was told to dismount and make room for a better man. He dismounted and planted himself at the butt of a tree within the line of guns.

The troop was now about to change its position, but as the writer did not see the force of being left on the field, he immediately betook himself to a seat on one of the limber-boxes, and beside him was placed the headless body of the poor major. The effect of the wound the writer had received now began to be felt; the loss of blood increased his thirst, but there was no water to be had, and the sight of the headless body certainly made his position anything but enviable, and he was compelled to relinquish his seat and look out for another. It was fortunate for him he did so; a second cannon shot severed the body he had just left in halves! Some of the gunners observing this, picked up the shattered remains, tied them up in a horse-blanket, and refastened them on the same box.

It was now getting dusk; the troop was in a frightfully crippled state from the loss it had sustained in men and horses, there being only a young lieutenant (W. A. Mackinnon) in charge. Still the troop advanced, and in the advance the writer took his seat on the trail of a wagon, and felt for a short time pretty comfortable. But only for a very short time: the gun on his right halted in consequence of its two pole-men being literally cut in two, the lower portions of their bodies still remaining in the saddle, the upper portion of the right pole-man's body being on the ground, while that of the left was suspended by the head over the collar-bar. The sergeant-major brought up a spare man to take the place of the near pole-man, at the same time emptying the two saddles of their ghastly burdens. It must be said that the spare man hesitated to jump into the saddle—for one of the mangled bodies was that of his brother!

The sergeant-major seeing there was no time to be lost, freed the collar-bar from the half body hanging over it, and threatened the spare gunner with his pistol if he did not jump into the saddle immediately, and he did so. The gun on the writer's left had now halted; the off pole-man having been struck by a round shot in the face, which carried away the left half, the body still sitting erect in the saddle. Here another spare man ran up, tilted the body out of the saddle, and sprang up into his seat, which he had scarcely attained when a shot broke the off fore-leg of the horse he had just mounted.

The horse was sent adrift, but appeared loth to leave his mates on the advance of the battery, for he hobbled after it, and as ill-luck would have it, came blundering up to the wagon, on the beam of which the writer was seated, and poked himself between the wheels of the limber and wagon, putting an end to all progress for a time. Holding on with his left arm, the writer tried his utmost to keep the brute off with his feet; but a cannon ball soon solved the difficulty. It struck the horse on the hind quarter, causing him to bound forward, and knock the writer off his perch, placing him in imminent danger of being run over.

There is one incident which may be worth relating here: prior to his being knocked off his seat, a ball struck the pole horse of the wagon on which the writer was seated, in the stomach, and in an instant the poor animal's intestines were hanging about its leg. The writer called to the rider informing him of the mishap in language more plain than refined perhaps by saying "Tom! Tom!" (the man's name was Tom Connolly) "Snarly Yow" (the horse's name) "has turned inside out, and his inwards are dangling about!"

Tom shouted to the corporal leading the team, "Joe! Joe! pull up! Snarly's g—ts are hanging about his legs!"

To which request the corporal coolly made answer: "Be gorra, Tom, I wouldn't pull up at such a time as this if you're own g—ts were hanging out!"

The writer was afterwards told that the horse did not drop until the troop formed battery again at a considerable distance to the right. The enemy's cavalry could be seen hanging about at no great distance so it was hopeless for him to attempt to procure another seat, the troop having broken into a gallop to avoid the enemy's cavalry charging them, so he was left behind to himself among his dead comrades, and being in great pain, and much in need of rest, he was fain to lay himself down by the side of the dead horse which had caused his second mishap, and screen himself, the best way he could, from the view of the enemy's cavalry; for they showed no mercy to the wounded.

He must have remained here till about midnight, when he was considerably astonished at hearing, no great distance off, the voices of Europeans. He gladly hailed them, and found them to be wounded infantry-men on their way to the rear—if they could find it. As a matter of course, the writer joined them, but as none of them had the slightest idea of their whereabouts, or where they were wandering (for it was pitch dark) they made up their minds to halt under the first tree they came across. They found one shortly, and made another discovery, namely, that they were not out of the range of the enemy's fire, for the tree was struck several times during their stay under it.

They were not, however, very long here when they heard

the rumbling sound of wheels, and remained perfectly silent to discover, if possible, whether those advancing were friends or foes. Happily they proved the former; it was Hereford's 9-pounder battery, which had marched out with us from Umballa. Here the writer met with old friends, who had known him when he was a boy serving with them in the same battalion of Foot Artillery—The Fighting 4th. Several of his companions were found dead under the tree which had sheltered them; they had died from sheer loss of blood and want of water. Such of them as were alive were accommodated on the wagons, and taken on to the main body of the artillery headquarters, from whence the recall was sounded by order of Brigadier Brookes, in order, if possible to assemble all the artillery together for the night.

Here were found all the troops of horse artillery, with the exception of the writer's own; being questioned about the troop's whereabouts, he could only answer up to the time he had left it—or rather, it had left him. There was a well here, which was surrounded by hundreds of thirsty souls, all patiently waiting their turn for a drink, the writer's share consisting of a handful of mud, from which he in vain endeavoured to extract some moisture. The mud he placed into his wound, which seemed to stanch the bleeding somewhat, and then laid himself down on the softest bit of earth he could find with his head between the spokes of a gun-wheel for a pillow and tried to get a little sleep.

This, however, was impossible, in consequence of the pain of the wound and the severity of the cold till daybreak. He ascertained, subsequently, that his troop had, during the night, strayed away under the enemy's entrenchments, so close as to be within pistol shot, which, of course, prevented them from replying to the bugles which had been sounded during the night to recall it. Meanwhile, it was generally reported among the other troops of horse artillery, that the "second of the first" had been cut up to a man.

At daybreak on the 22nd, the troop was discovered, simultaneously by us and by the enemy, who immediately opened fire on it. They were unable to return the enemy's fire, their ammunition being quite exhausted, and the horses, jaded and fagged beyond measure; the second set of horses with the six spare ammunition wagons (well stocked), drawn by bullocks, could not be found in the night.

The troop was rescued from its more than perilous position by the despatch of another troop of horse artillery to its relief, and strange to say the enemy's fire had no effect on either of our batteries. The only way in which this bad practice of the enemy can be accounted for is, that during the night their heavy guns were in an entrenched camp, and they kept up their fire all night. They, perhaps, never thought of running up their guns after each discharge, but allowed the trails to sink lower into the earth, which caused too great an elevation of the gun's muzzles to produce any effect on our guns, though they were quite within range of the enemy's fire.

At dawn, on the 22nd, the action was recommenced by the horse artillery again advancing to the front, the writer's troop having rejoined the left wing under Sir Henry Hardinge, and here the writer planted himself on one of the gun-seats of the third troop, rather than be left behind. Here, again, he was told by Major Swinley, commanding the troop, that he "was in the way and must vacate his seat." This annoyed him considerably, and on his asking Major Swinley if he really intended leaving him behind, he was politely introduced by that officer to the notice of Brigadier Brookes, who ordered him to mount a spare horse of his own troop, and find the best of his way, in company with a mounted *syce*, to Ferozepore, a distance of ten miles.

On the road all the spare horses of the troop were seen each mounted by a *syce*, and the six spare ammunition wagons, well stocked, drawn by bullocks which had been so much wanted on the previous night. They had all been carefully kept well to the rear, and had never been under the range of fire. Numbers of our wounded cavalry and infantry soldiers

BATTLE OF FEROZESHAH, DECEMBER 21-21, 1845

were seated on elephants making their way to the same place for which the writer was bound, besides hundreds of native soldiery (unwounded), who had apparently no taste for the hard work going on in front, and were marching to Ferozepore, amusing themselves as they marched by firing their ammunition in the air. On our march were seen one or two wells, and the sepoys freely indulging in refreshing draughts of water, easily obtained by them with their bundles of cordage and their lotahs, but they positively declined to give the unfortunate Europeans on the elephants a drink, unless they paid for it!

The writer not being in possession of the *quid pro quo*—in other words, having nothing to give,—both himself and his horse had to go without. On entering the fort at Ferozepore, about noon on the 22nd, he made his way to a well where he found a trough full of water for cattle. Here both his horse and himself drank eagerly. The refreshment was surely deserved, for both had been since three o'clock on the morning of the 21st without a drop of water! No man can estimate even his own powers of endurance until he is taught by experience what he can do in this way—or any other.

Here, too, he met two ladies; friends he had known at Umballa, who took him to their small tent, and were exceedingly kind. From thence he proceeded to the hospital, where he found the medical men with their shirt-sleeves tucked up, busily at work in the open air. On his presenting himself, he was directed to take a seat, and every preparation made for amputating his arm from the shoulder. Seeing this, he declined the pleasure of being winged, and was promptly told that if he did not choose to submit to that form of treatment, he might go to the deuce and treat himself.

He returned to the ladies he had left; they were glad that he had refused to have his arm amputated, and set off in search of a native doctor, who speedily made his appearance, and with the assistance of the ladies his wound was dressed, to his infinite relief. They were good enough to insist upon his making use of their bed, and he speedily sank into a slumber which lasted several hours, and from which he awoke like a giant refreshed! Having been without sleep or rest for the previous 60 hours.

Late in the afternoon of the 22nd a great panic arose in the fort, where all the ladies and soldiers' wives belonging to the troops stationed at Ferozepore were located during the fighting. This panic was caused by the rumour (with its thousand tongues) that the British had been beaten, and the Sikhs were advancing to take the fort.

The writer saw an officer, apparently commandant of the fort, (indeed he was big enough to command half a dozen,) armed to the teeth, a huge pair of pistols fastened round his anything but dandy waist (he must have measured four feet round the stomach), a drawn sword in one hand, and an enormous telescope in the other, running frantically about, shouting, "Artillery men! artillery men! stand to your guns—the enemy are upon us!"

A great cloud of dust had been seen approaching from the direction of the battle field, and the soldiers who had been left to defend the fort were instantly at their posts, the wounded being all got together, for they were utterly helpless. The alarm however was groundless; the commandant made out, through the agency of his extensive telescope, that the dust was caused by the various escorts bringing in the captured guns, ammunition, &c, and the wounded. It was a great relief to all, and Daniel Lambert (the Commandant) returned from his post of observation, with as jaunty a step, and as bright a smile on his fat old face as if he had won a victory and been decorated with the Grand Cross of the Bath.

The wounded, some on carts, some on elephants, (indeed all kinds of conveyance had to be improvised for their accommodation), were brought into the hospital tents in the fort. The sights there to be seen were most harrowing. Most of the writer's comrades of the horse artillery who were taken out of the carts had died on the field from loss of blood and scarcity of water, and some of them were at the door of death, gasping their last. They were all placed side by side on the ground; several of them had their limbs shattered with round shot and grape; and after the moribund had breathed their last, they were again put into carts, and taken outside the fort to be buried in a pit dug for the purpose ; a great many had been injured by the explosion of the charged mines employed by the Sikhs, and it was heart-rending to see the carnage and destruction of human life which was seen in the fort of Ferozepore on that 22nd December 1845.

It was not till the 22nd and 24th instant that regular hospitals were established for the several branches of the service in cantonments. The writer went, of course, to the artillery hospital, where all his hurts were attended to. He had leisure to look up his troop, which he found had come on to Ferozepore and had just returned from burying the commanding officer's remains in the cemetery.

This brief sketch closes the writer's experience of Ferozshuhur. And these experiences—let the reader judge of what nature they were—were sustained without a morsel of food, a drop of water or a tot of grog. Certain is he that if grog had been in question he could not have escaped as he did, but must have inevitably had to give up from sheer fatigue, loss of blood, and thirst.

He gives here, for want of his own personal reminiscences of the mere fighting, extracts from an authentic and excellent account of what occurred about midnight of the 21st.

> At midnight the enemy again opened a destructive fire in the dark; on this the governor-general mounted his horse, and called on the 80th (Staffordshire) Regiment, which was at the head of the column: "My lads! No sleep for us, until we take those guns." The battalion immediately deployed and advanced, supported by the 1st Bengal Europeans (now the 101st Fusiliers), drove a large body of Sikhs from their guns, Which they spiked, falling back as steadily

as if on parade. The gallant 80th took up its position at the head of the column, their steady appearance winning the admiration of the Commander-in-Chief, who exclaimed, as the men passed him: "Plucky dogs! Plucky dogs! We cannot fail to win with such men as these!"

The remainder of the night passed with an occasional cannonading from the enemy. Sir Hugh Gough and Sir Henry Hardinge resolved to keep the ground they were in possession of, and await the coming dawn to attack the batteries of the enemy, if they still manned them, or, as a dernier ressort, to take them in reverse, and conquer or die. If ever troops were inspired with the most perfect confidence in their leaders, it was ours at Ferozshuhur, under the gallant Sir Hugh, so kind of heart, and so heroically brave, and the veteran Hardinge. Right well they knew that the struggle would be a hard one, but they cheered every one round them with the certainty of victory.

Save his son, Arthur Hardinge, who had a horse killed under him, all the staff of the governor-general had been killed or wounded.

"The night of the 21st was the most extraordinary of my life," wrote the latter, in a letter to his family. "I bivouacked with the men, without food or covering, and our nights are bitterly cold. A burning camp in our front, our brave fellows lying down under a heavy cannonade, mixed with the wild cries of the Sikhs, our British hurrahs, the tramp of men and the groans of the dying. In this state, with a handful of men, who had carried the batteries during the night, I remained till morning, taking very short intervals of rest by lying down with various regiments in succession, to ascertain their temper and revive their spirits."

Daylight saw the British troops deploying into line. Sir Hugh rode thirty yards in front of the right, and the governor-general the same distance in front of the left to prevent the men from firing as they advanced against the Sikh batteries. So, steadily, and compact as a living wall, the line advanced without firing a shot, although horse artillery on the flanks and our heavy guns in the centre, opened an effective fire, to which were added flights of rockets, which hurtled swiftly through the air with a terrible sound. A masked battery of the Sikhs responded, dismantling some of our central guns, and blowing up the timbrels. Here it was that all our first troop 1st brigade had their wagons blown up.

The opposition was but slight, most of the enemy's guns being taken in reverse, and wheeling round past the village of Ferozeshah, the British line came round with a mighty sweep, its bayonets shining like a moving' hedge of steel, down the whole left and rear of the enemy's position, halting when they had cleared the works at the opposite extremity, completely dislodging the enemy.

"The line," says the despatch, "then halted as on a day of manoeuvre, receiving its two leaders as they rode along the front with a most gratifying cheer, and displaying the captured standards of the Khulsá army. We had taken upwards of seventy-three pieces of cannon, and were masters of the whole field."

"The loss of the army has been heavy," reported Sir Hugh Gough: "how could a hope be formed that it would be otherwise? Within thirty-four hours this force stormed an entrenched camp, fought a general action, and sustained two considerable combats with the enemy; within four days it has dislodged from their positions on the left bank of the Sutlej 60,000 Sikh soldiers supported by 150 pieces of cannon, 108 of which they acknowledge to have lost, and 91 of which are in our possession. Among the captured guns were found two horse artillery guns (six-pounders) which were originally presented to Runjeet Singh by Lord Auckland, when Governor-Genera! of India."

Our total loss was 694 killed and 4,721 wounded: of the latter 595 died, or were totally disabled for life. The battle over, every exertion was made to alleviate the condition and ameliorate the sufferings of the wounded.

The writer must now return to the hospital, where he found himself quartered with about 120 of his comrades of the Bengal Artillery. We were visited on many occasions by Sir Henry Hardinge, who had a kind and cheering word for everyone. If a poor fellow had lost an arm, the Governor-General would point to his own empty sleeve, and remind him that he had lost an arm at Ligny in 1815; if another had lost a leg he would remind him that one of his sons, who was by his side in battle, had lost a foot, and the poor fellows, were so delighted that they forgot their sufferings for a time, completely carried away by soldierly urbanity of the Peninsular veteran, who was the arbiter of the destinies of India.

The writer's hospital comrade (a soldier was nobody in those days, unless he had a comrade, no matter where he was or what he was doing) was a gunner of his old battalion of Foot Artillery, the 4th—who had been brought into hospital the previous day in a most deplorable condition, he having been blown away from his own gun, accidentally, in the dark, and had been left for dead on the field for two days and nights. He was picked up with all his clothes burnt off his body, nothing remaining un-burnt but his boots; his left hand shattered to fragments, and his left eye gone. The arm was amputated just below the elbow, and it is gratifying to know, and to remember, that after all his disintegration he survived to reach his native land (Old Ireland,) with a good pension.

As Sir Henry approached this poor fellow's bed—he had what our great mimic called a "jocative" remark for him, pointing to his own empty sleeve the while, as much as to say—"There's a pair of us, as the devil said to his knee-buckles;" and on looking up to the writer's bed-head ticket, he said: "You are very young to be so severely wounded; would you like to have satisfaction my lad?"

An affirmative reply was given, the reader may be sure. A few beds further on he saw a much younger lad, who was wounded by a grape shot which had passed through both cheeks. He said to him, "well, my lad, I see you have two beauty-spots on your face to take home to your sweetheart."

The youngster abruptly said, "I have no sweetheart!"

"That's quare," said the governor-general, "I thought soldiers and sailors had sweethearts wherever they went! But never mind, my boy, if you haven't you will have, and that's some consolation. You won't be the worse thought of though for having a little less cheek than usual."

This was Christmas Eve, and Sir Henry in going round overheard one wounded man say to another "tomorrow will be Christmas day, but I'm afraid we shall have no mince pies."

"That you shall, my good fellow," said Sir Henry, and on the morrow more than a thousand of the coveted dainties were distributed among the wounded. All who were able mightily enjoyed the luxury—consuming not only their own share, but the share of those who were unable to do so and washed them down with libations of cold water or tea—nothing stronger could be had—quaffed to the health of the kind-hearted Sir Henry.

A day or two afterwards we had rum, beer and wine issued to us in medicinal proportion, and we were fed like any number of fighting cocks to make up for our previous fasting. Sleep, however, was denied us. What with pain, evil dreams of the past, and the moans of the dying, the nights were something dreadful to pass, and even horrible to remember. Such as were able would endeavour to while away the bitter hours by recounting little historiettes of their lives; others would sing a verse or two of some favourite old ditty, until the hour arrived at which sleeping draughts were issued, and each man got his dose and did his best to court "Tired Nature's soft Restorer."

Such was the daily routine in the hospital. Some recovered, and rejoined their corps and companies to be ready for another set-to with the enemy; numbers died; others were invalided and sent home to England, and the remnant detailed for a change to the hills, till the hospital was finally broken up in March 1846. The writer was of the number sent out to join his troop, and to his great horror he was sent back to the same hospital after the battle of Sobraon, his wound having broken out afresh.

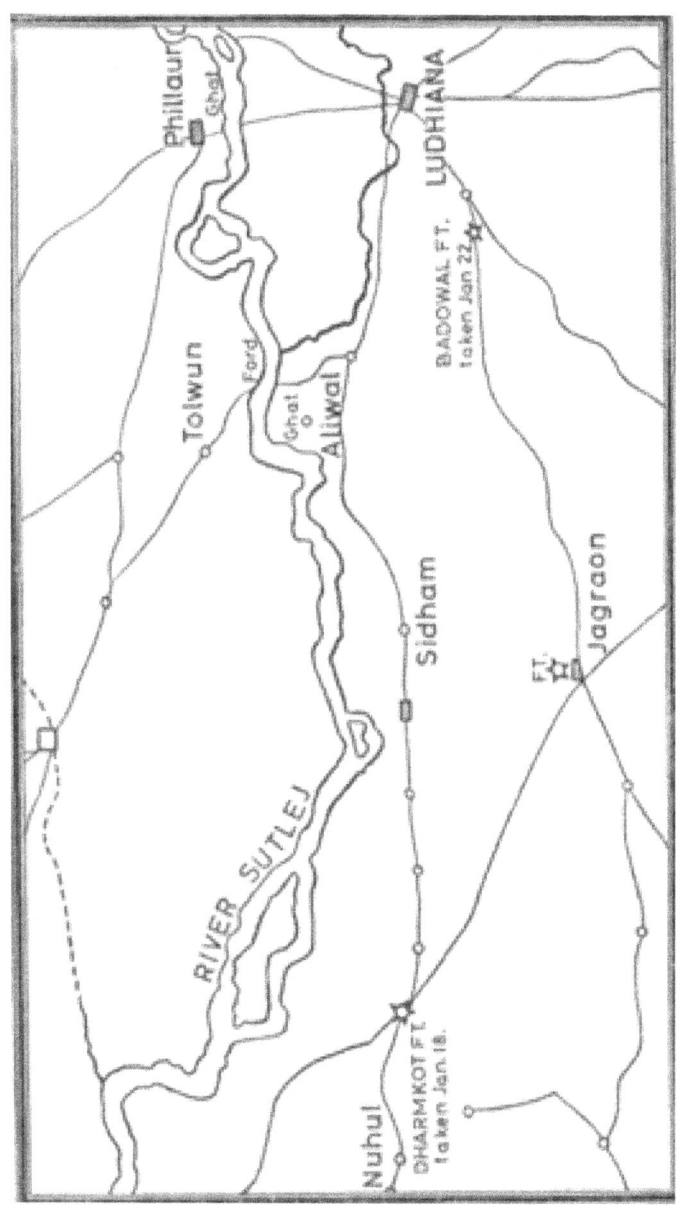

Sir Harry Smith's Movements in January 1846

CHAPTER 6

Aliwal

The battle of Aliwal, which was fought on the 28th of January 1846, forms so brilliant an episode in the Sutlej Campaign, that this history would be incomplete, indeed, were it omitted, but the troop to which the writer belonged was not present to share the glory shed upon the British arms that day. He has been at some pains to compile from authentic and trustworthy sources the account which follows. It is only second-hand, it is true, but, as the Irishman said when he turned his coat twice, "One good turn deserves another," and the writer hopes his version will pass current; the information from which it has been obtained being quite as reliable as that given by any historian, ancient or modern.

By the discomfited military Sikh leaders the utmost pains were taken to conceal the losses they had sustained from the Sikh Durbar, and the greatest excitement and anxiety prevailed in Lahore, as it was naturally supposed our troops would follow up their advantages and march on the capital; but without a siege train, and more European troops, cavalry especially, this movement could not be attempted. It was therefore resolved to wait for the siege train, which was advancing with H.M'.s 9th and 16th Lancers, 10th and 53rd Regiments of Infantry, which, with the 43rd and 59th Native Infantry, had composed the Meerut force under Sir John Grey, K.C.B.

Encouraged by this delay, the Sikhs resolved to make another effort to hold their ground on the left bank of the Sutlej; and began to construct a pontoon bridge, not far from the spot where they had crossed the river after the battle of Ferozshuhur, and our army being at some little distance, no opposition was offered to them.

They speedily constructed a bridge of boats. Above this bridge there was a good ford and advantage was soon taken of the extreme weakness, in point of numbers, of our troops at Ludianah. No attack was made upon the town or cantonment, the object of the Sikhs being apparently to entrench themselves near the point where they had passed the river, in order to obstruct our progress, and cut off, if possible, supplies en route, to our posts at Ferozepore.

As soon, however, as Sir John Grey's column came in from Meerut, measures were immediately adopted to reinforce our post at Ludianah, and that at Busseau. Some native infantry, light cavalry, and artillery were sent to both places, while the sick, and the women and children, were despatched to Umballa. Sir Henry Hardinge truly said of India, that (as indeed he might have said of anywhere,) "It is a country where it is impossible to say on one day what the next may bring forth." But there, in war time, every day ushered ill something new and stirring.

When the army had thus been lightened of a multitude of its followers, Sir Harry Smith, (the comrade of the brave Moore at Coruña) had with him 7,000 men and 24 pieces of cannon, with which it was estimated he could relieve Ludianah and cover our entire rear.

At daybreak on the 28th of January, the force commanded by Sir Harry Smith began to move against the enemy's position. He had the cavalry in front riding in contiguous column of squadrons, and two troops of horse artillery in the intervals of brigades. Then came the infantry, in contiguous columns of brigades, at deploying distance, artillery in the intervals, followed by two eight-inch howitzers, such was Sir Harry's order of march; Brigadier Godby's Brigade on the right, the

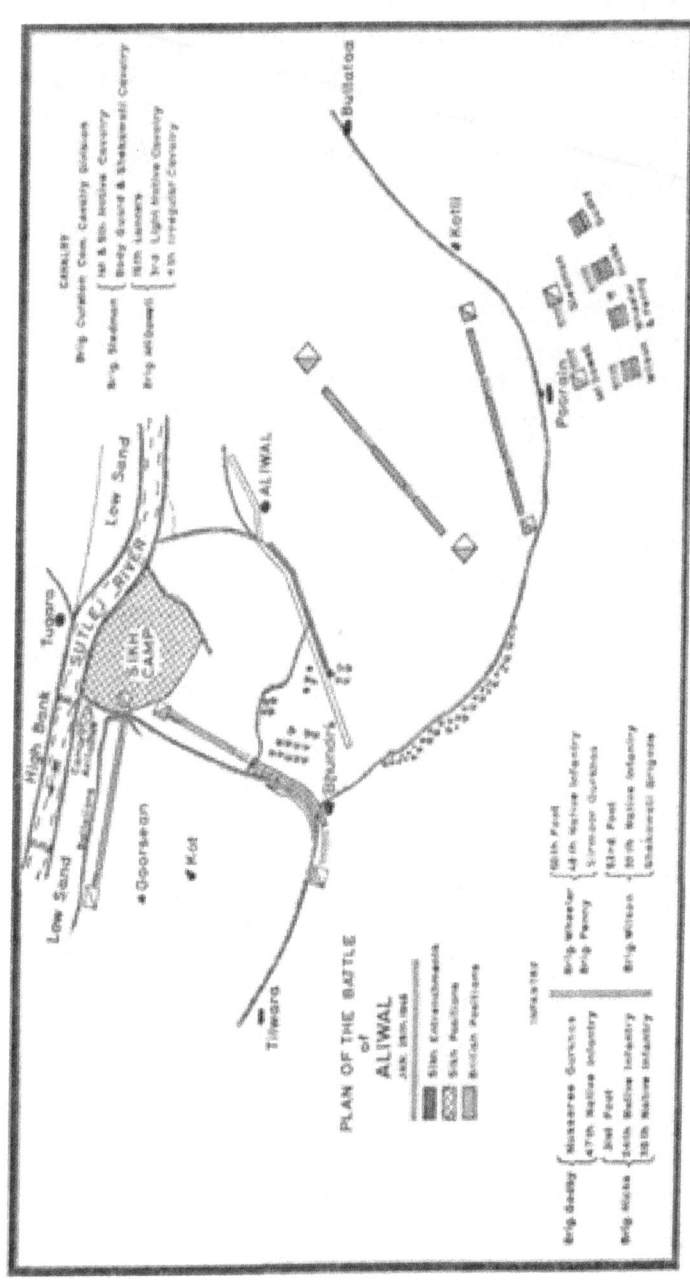

Battle of Aliwal, January 28th, 1846

Shekawatta Infantry on the left, and the 4th Irregular Cavalry extended far away on the right, "For the purpose of sweeping," his despatch states, "the banks of a wet *nullah* on the right, and preventing any of the enemy's horse attempting an inroad towards Ludianah, or an attempt upon our baggage, which was assembled round the foot of Budhowal. My advance was steady; my troops well in hand, and if the evening had not anticipated me on the Jugeaon road, I could have fallen upon his centre with advantage."

From the summit of a house in the village of Pooreia Sir Harry, through his telescope, first had a distant view of the Sikhs. By the glittering of their arms they were evidently to motion in front, along a ridge, of which the little village of Aliwal (a name destined to be remembered in all ages where our language is spoken) seemed to be the centre. Runjoon Singh's left appeared still to occupy its ground in the circular entrenchment near the river, but his right had been brought; forward, and occupied the ridge, with Boondree on one flank and Aliwal on the other, a ford of the Sutlej being in rear of the whole.

The cavalry, the 16th Lancers, their parti-coloured pennons fluttering, and their magnificent appearance exciting the admiration of all who saw them, friend or foe; the Irregular Horse, in dark-blue and gold; the 1st Light Cavalry, &c, &c, in the well-known inevitable silver-grey trimmed with scarlet, of the company's service, deployed by squadrons into line, and moved on easily, as the ground was perfectly open, hard and covered with grass. The horse artillery dressed in their usual leather breeches and long boots, and their uniform of blue trimmed with scarlet and gold, took ground, gradually to the right and left as they advanced, thus covering the heads of the infantry columns, which now also deployed into line, steadily, with bayonets fixed and colours flying. The artillery were massed on the flanks and in the centre; there was no dust, for the country round about was green and grassy, and the January sun shone with almost unclouded brilliance; hence, when

BATTLE OF SOBRAON, FEBRUARY 10, 1846

the army, on an attempt of Runjoon Singh to turn its flank, broke into open column again to take ground to the right, "manoeuvres, which," Sir Harry states, "were performed with the precision of the most correct field-day, the battle was most imposing."

The line again advanced, but had scarcely done so for 150 yards, when, at 10 o'clock, a.m., the Sikhs opened a furious cannonades along their whole front. At first the balls fell short, and only lodged in, or furrowed up, the turf, tearing long, deep ruts ; then they reached us, and men and horses began to fall on every side, in most instances to rise no more, for few ever survive a wound from a cannon shot. Though under this fire, Sir Harry now halted the whole line till he could ascertain whether, by carrying the village of Aliwal, he could, with effect, throw himself upon Runjoon's left and centre. The idea was scarcely conceived ere it was executed by the brigades of Godby and Hicks, which, by one rapid and furious rush, carried the village and two guns of great calibre. This was the key to the whole position.

Again a gleam of light seemed to pass along the ridges of steel bayonets as the line advanced once more, H. M.'s 31st Foot, and the native regiments, emulous for the front, and ere long the battle became general; the roar of musketry rang from flank to flank along the open ground and up the ridge crowned by the hostile Sikhs, the smoke being so dense that the colours could only be seen at times in the intervals of firing!

As the Sikhs had a strong body of cavalry on the ridge to their left, Brigadier Cureton with our right brigade of dragoons dashed in among them with resolute gallantry and hurled them in confused masses back upon their infantry, while a noble charge was made in another direction by the Light Cavalry and the Bodyguard. "The Shekawattee Brigade was moved well on to the right in support of Cureton, when I observed the enemy's encampment," said our chief, "and saw that it was full of infantry. I immediately brought upon it

Godby's brigade, by changing front, and taking the enemy's infantry in reverse. They drove these before them, and took some guns without a check."

While these brilliant movements were taking place upon our right and the enemy's left, between the village and the sandy banks of the Sutlej, Brigadier Wheeler might have been seen advancing with his column like a scarlet flood, charging with the bayonet through fire and smoke, carrying guns and everything before it, deploying again into line, and again moving on, in a manner which ably displayed the coolness of the Brigadier and the gallantry of his irresistible brigade composed of H. M.'s 50th Foot, the 48th Native Infantry, and the Sirmoor Battalion. On the left the 53rd, or Shropshire Regiment, with the 30th Native Infantry, whose dark countenances contrasted curiously with their pale buff facings, equalled their comrades on the right by the fury and celerity with which they flung themselves on the battalions of the enemy.

The Sikhs now being well driven back on the left and centre, strove hard to hold their right to secure the passage of the river; and for that purpose strongly occupied the village of Boondree. To drive them thence a squadron of our 16th Lancers (a Corps which by the way first came to India in 1822, and had fought at Calpee and Bhurtpore, and were now clad in scarlet) advanced under Major Smith and Captain Pearson. The former received a wound, but led his squadron gallantly to the right of the village, bearing and spearing everything before them, and going right through and through a square of infantry, using the lance with the most deadly effect.

The Sikhs threw themselves on the ground, so that sometimes the lancers failed to reach them in charging past, and were fired on from the rear, when the Sikhs sprang to their feet—in some cases they flung away their muskets—and like the Highland clansmen of old, flung themselves with their keen swords and round-shields upon the horsemen. In these charges the 16th had eight officers and upwards of 100 troops killed and wounded. Their charge at Boondree was ably sustained by the 3rd Bengal Cavalry, led by Major Angelo.

There, the largest gun upon the field, and seven others, were captured, while the gallant Shropshires stormed the village with the bayonet, and the 30th Native Infantry swept round its rear with invincible spirit. Two troops of horse artillery, led by Major Lawrenson, now dashed at full speed (the gun-wheels crushing dead and wounded alike) among the flying masses of the enemy, into which they sent their plunging fire of round shot and grape until about a thousand of them rallied in fierce and sullen desperation under shelter of the bank of a *nullah*, and then, facing about, opened a heave fire. A charge was made by the 30th Native Infantry, who drove the foe back, and then rustled among the troops of Avitabile, driving them from the bank of the river with yells and shouts, and exposing them once more to a deadly fire from twelve of our horse artillery guns, at less than 300 yards, and when a junction was effected with the 53rd Foot from the right of the village, the battle of Aliwal was won!

Our troops were all advancing with the bayonet, and firing steadily the while, in the most perfect order, as if to one common focus, the passage of the river, while, flying before them, the enemy were completely hemmed in, and wildly flinging themselves in disordered masses into the ford and in boats, in confusion and consternation, while our eight-inch howitzers pitched shell after shell into them without interruption.

Ere long the debris of the Sikh army was seen to spread along the opposite and higher bank of the river, but flying still in every direction, although a sort of line was endeavoured to be formed to cover their retreat, till all our guns opened upon them, and then the vaunted irresistible, unconquered army, became converted into a mere demoralized rabble, and literally seemed to melt away. They had succeeded in drawing only two of their cannon to the opposite bank, where they were spiked, one by Lieutenant Holmes, of the Irregular Cavalry, and the other by Gunner Scott, of the Horse Artillery, who rode through the river for the purpose. Many stuck fast in the Sutlej, midway across, and two men, who unfortunately got among the quicksands, vanished for ever. Save these two guns, every gun of the enemy fell into our hands, and thirty jingals attached to Avitabile's corps were taken.

Headlong the Sikhs were driven in a terrified multitude over a most difficult ford of a broad river, while camp baggage, stores of ammunition, grain, and spoil of every description, were wrested from them. All this was accomplished by repeated charges of horse and foot, our howitzers and guns being always ahead of everything! So said the despatches, as also MacGregor's History of the Sikhs. Our grand total of killed, wounded, and missing, was 589 men and 353 horses.

Major Lawrenson, of the horse artillery, reported that the quantity of captured ammunition, consisting of shot, shell, grape, and ball-cartridge was "beyond accurate calculation." Gorgeous shawls, of which an Empress might be proud; bracelets and bangles of gold; gilded shields and swords (magnificent blades the latter) were "thick as the leaves in Vallambrosa," and fell in showers into the hands of the victors. The Sikhs perished in vast numbers on the field, but many more in their despairing efforts to cross the river.

They had proved themselves to be the most brave, fierce, and determined, not to say obstinate enemies, we had yet encountered in India. To a great extent they had the advantage of military discipline and the regimental systems taught them by those French and Italian soldiers of fortune who had served Runjeet Singh the old Lion of Lahore, and who laid the foundation of their high reputation. Even the Afghans were little in the field as compared with the Sikhs, whose natural courage was kept always inflamed by large doses of opium, bhang, and other maddening drugs, which rendered them alike incapable of fear or mercy, and converted them into perfect fiends. They fired into our wounded as they lay helpless on the ground, or hacked them to pieces with their swords, in short, they had all the foulest vices which disgrace the majority of Asiatic nations.

CHAPTER 7

Standing Camp

Now for a line or two about camp life, now that we have got the Sikhs on the run. The reader must understand that there are two kinds of camps, a moving, and a standing. Attached to the former a soldier is in his glory: it is full of life; fresh scenery, daily; enough of exercise to do him good and excite a most outrageous appetite, which he has the wherewithal to gratify, unless perhaps in time of war. The very marching itself is delightful; then there is the hurry and bustle of striking and pitching the tents, the arrangements for picketing the horses, packing the guns, &c, the wondering what sort of a road it will turn out; what sort of camp-ground the next will be, and so on. In a standing camp (although be it said there are ample means of enjoyment—if one could but get them) the rule is quite the reverse of its peripatetic confrere. A standing camp, the writer has found, begins and ends with a life of the utmost monotony. We pitched our camp once more after the battle of Ferozeshah, on or about the 25th of December, and did not strike tents again until after the battle of Sobraon, on the 10th of February.

But before touching on the engagement of Sobraon the writer is desirous of saying a word or two on the vexed question of grog,—which has been the cause of more crime than any other cause known and the irreparable ruin of some of the finest men in the artillery, or in the service, dragging young and old, men, women and grown children into its vortex. A powerful factor in every species of rascality, blackguardom and sin is John Barleycorn. We had a man in our troop, a most amusing fellow, and an inveterate drunkard. When sober, he was all that a man should be; when he was tipsy, no greater brute ever walked on four legs, or "crawled, be gorra," as he used to say himself!

The change was marvellous. "You are a gentleman, sir," the commanding officer said to him, when he was had up for drunkenness on one occasion, "when you are sober, when you are drunk you belong to the lowest class of *mehters*—a *dhome* in fact! Faugh! I'm ashamed of you! What have you to say?"

"Well, sir," said Barney, who was a great favourite, and could take liberties for which another would be wheeled, "you see, sur, av drink didn't change a man, divil a use in takin' it! Sorra bit o' me knows how it happens, bud it always happens wid me! I'm not meself at all! Did ivir ye hear a line or two av an ould ditty we used to sing at home, they call John Barleycorn, sur: about what drink will make a man do, sur?"

The captain frowned at Barney and said, "we don't wish to hear any such trash—here."

"Oh! then," said Barney, "av ye think it's me wud be openin' me gob to sing in tho Orderly Room and the Major in it—not to spake of yerself,—av coorse," and the least shadow of sarcasm crept into his voice as he said the words, (and the captain was not slow to perceive it.)

"We don't want singing" said the major, "but he might repeat the words. Can you?" he said to the culprit.

"Deed an' I can that" said Barney—"aye faith and sing id tu."

"Repeat the words," said the major, interrupting him.

"I will, sur," said Barney, and screwing up his face into a most laughter-moving succession of wrinkles, he began—

John Barleycorn was the finest grain-
That ivir was grown on Ian';
It could make a man do any thing;
Be the waverin' av his han'
Be the waverin' av his han'!

(And here he interjaculated "Sorra lie in id!")

It could make a mar' become a mule;
A mule become an ass;
It could tern gold into silver,
Aye—an' silver into brass!
Be the waverin' av his han'!

"And," said Barney, "that's what he does wid me!"

This "elegant extract" was destined to get Barney off scot-free upon the occasion which is referred to; whether it was Barney's face, or his voice, or as that gentleman called it, "the strength av the poethry," that excited the chief's risible faculties, this deponent sayeth not, but be the cause what it might, it had the effect of throwing him, and indeed all present, into convulsions of laughter, under cover of which Barney was released, much to his own astonishment and that of his comrades, who had quite made up their mind that they were about to be deprived of Barney's delightful society for some little time. Crude as Barney's poetry may be it conveys pretty accurately the effect that grog has upon most men.

At the time written about, the whole artillery regiment had only three canteens, and rum was the only liquor sold therein the price of which was one *anna* per dram, and if you were luxurious, and wished your raw material refined a little, and converted into punch, another half anna produced the desired effect, per tot, and so liberal were the regulations on the subject that a man was allowed to drink as much as he was able to pay for.

The canteen stations were Dum-Dum (the then headquarters of the regiment) Cawnpore and Meerut, and all detached troops and companies had their rum, viz., two drams per man, issued to them immediately after morning parade, on an empty stomach. The old soldiers—hardened, and saddened, if the expression can be used—preferred the rum to their breakfast; the younger ones preferred the latter. The first instalment was termed a gum tickler; the second a gall burster. After swallowing the two drams of rum, all hands sat down to a hearty breakfast; and it was always observed that those who had taken the rum, did not eat so hearty a breakfast as those who had gone without the liquor.

Those who did not care to drink the rum to which they were entitled, allowed a class of men, who were called *bagdadders* (rum-dealers) to draw their allowance for a month at the rate of *Rs*. 8, or two *annas* a dram, thereby clearing a nett profit of 100 *per cent*, on the month's grog transaction, while others took their rum away in bottles, and either consumed it themselves in the day, or sold it to souls more thirsty than themselves, at a charge of four *annas* per dram, making a clear profit of 300 *per cent*, on every tot they sold. This nefarious practice was carried on with impunity, although not recognized by the officers, but winked at all the same, not only in the artillery but in every regiment, horse or foot, in Her Majesty's or the Company's service.

Matters are much mended now, but in the days of which the writer treats, the issue of grog itself, and the clandestine manner in which it was acquired and disposed of, reflected the greatest disgrace, not only on the parties to the transaction, but on those who possessed the power of putting a slop to such proceedings and who neglected to do so. The great contrast between the restrictions on the sale of liquor now and then, and the admirable manner in which all such nefarious traffic is now stamped out, has urged the writer to allude to the question, and he congratulates the men of every regiment in the service, the young hands, that is, that they did not serve in his time!

But to come back to the camp life. As has been said our tents were pitched, for the first time since Moodkee was fought, about 15 miles from Ferozeshah, and twenty-five miles from Ferozepore. A very short time sufficed to pull ourselves together, look after our traps, repair damages, and get ready to break out in a fresh place. The routine of duties, suspended for awhile by duties of greater moment, recommenced; training young horses, packing ammunition, changing guns which had been rendered unserviceable by the enemy's fire, guard-mounting, stable duty, a little drill, to set the young fellows up, and what is called square their shoulders to the front—"Chin well of the stock"!

Did ever any of my readers wear a stock of the style, manner, and pattern of that in use in the year of grace 1846? It is to be hoped not. A more ingenious method of torture a soldier never put his head into, and the blessing of a devout man (meaning the writer), will follow to the grave the man, or men, who were the cause of its abolition. The stiff, choking abomination was the cause of more cursing than that caused by the losing or gaining of all the stock sold on the Exchange.

Well, in this camp of ours, with all our arduous (?) duties, it fell out that with the plethora of grog a number of accomplishments developed themselves which had much better have been undeveloped. There was long bullets along the roads outside of camp; there was quoit pitching, close by, and there was a great deal of card playing in almost every tent in the lines between those who had made a little loot, (and their name was legion) and their less fortunate neighbours. But however the balance was struck, either by winner or loser, John Barleycorn stepped in at the heel of the hunt and claimed the stakes as his own.

The state of affairs, *re* grog, after Moodkee, changed the dispositions of a great many of our men ; and enhanced the price of the raw material. The *bagdadding* rate then current in the market rose steadily from four to eight *annas* per dram which was the culminating and ruling price while the produce of the loot lasted, although the writer has seen in the field *rupees* placed one on top of the other, until the commissariat tot (or measure) was brimful—and whatever amount there might be was the equivalent of the full of the measure of the wonderful produce of the rum issuer's cask.

Men who had not been in the habit of either drawing or drinking their liquor, began to have a sneaking regard for it, whether from a more highly cultivated state of taste, or a desire to make money for the purpose of losing at card-playing, who can say, and withdrew their patronage from the *bagdadders*, and started business on their own account, each preserving his own particular share in his own particular bottle, as Barney Hennessy used to say (with a dry wink and a wry mouth) "to his own particular cheek." After Ferozeshah a further enhancement took place in the price of Mr. Barleycorn. He assumed such a phase of respectability that lie was quoted at prices varying from eight *annas* per dram to one *rupee*, ditto, and remained firm at that. Indeed, it became quite a luxury; and as luxuries are only to be obtained at high prices, Mr. John remained firmly at that quotation, and seemed likely to be set there.

The writer saw, shortly after Ferozeshah, one comrade produce a bag, containing probably fifty *rupees* to another comrade, and offer the contents for a bottle of rum which the producer had saved in, say, four days. But the would-be purchaser was taken in; as the chum who had saved the precious stuff said to him: "Phelim, me deer, I can have the pleasure of drinkin' me bottles av grog before the next 'wire in'" (which was his free and easy way of talking about a general engagement), "but I may nivir have the pleasure av spendin' the money; anyhow ye are welkim to a tot, 'whether or yes,' an sure that will divert the drooth aff ye this blissid Sunday mornin."

"Drink, man," said he, "av ye can't write, ye can make yer mark in that, anyhow. We," the old fellow continued, "had a sarjint in the troop wanst, who had been a lawyer's clerk, or a bailiff, or a barrister, divil a know I know what, but when he wanted a tot he would come to me and say, Barney, me buck, produce the evidence, and we'll examine wan witness. But he didn't stop at wan. Be gorra he examined the intire body of evidence, and left ne'er a witness in the box—I mane glass in the bottle!"

The writer would not have the reader suppose that the bare ration of two tots of rum per man was the cause of this rise in price. Private sales of liquor were made by the commissariat *gomasthas* to any extent, and these were the description of men who financially benefited most during the campaign. They would buy anything and sell anything they had to sell. They were attached to the regiments for the purpose of issuing rations to men and horses, and combining their pleasure with our business they made an uncommonly good thing of it; many of them having joined the department with not as many articles of wearing apparel on their back "as would dust a flute," as Barney used to say, and "bedad, luck at thim now."

"They bought me loot," continued Barney, "fer an owld song; an' be the crass on an asses back, and that's thrue fer you anyhow, av I wint to thim fur a tot widout the pice, they wouldn't allow me to come widin the roar of an ass av thim! Bud, sure, when me awn comrades wud do the same, what's the use an wonderin' what a black fellow wud do!"

These *gomasthas* possessed facilities for disposing of loot, of which they were not slow to take advantage. How they contrived to get rid of it, consisting as it did of miscellaneous articles, extending from an elephant to a sable beauty's nose-ring, was a mystery and a wonder! In rear of the commissariat tent, day by day, even on the line of march, a string of hackeries might be seen, parked like our guns, with regularity and precision. The rations issued, and the loot sold and delivered, and the grog handed over (these gentry seldom gave cash) the string of *hackeries*, like the great Sikh army, gradually melted away and vanished into thin air. What they retained was safely bestowed among the commissariat stores, and, as Barney Hennessy said "he wud be a quare ould prize agent wud take them out o' that whether or no! See me now, av I haven't sowld things to that ould *gomaster* (the divil sweep him) that av I had in Tipperary town wud be a fortin' to me, for a bottle o' grog; an' now when ' it is too late to spare when all is spint'—dy'e mind now—be dam' av he'll give me a tot, av me tongue was hangin' out o' me hid the lingth av a yard or two! I don't wish him any harm," continued Barney, "but," drawing himself up to his full height, and smoothing his immense moustache down with the palm of his hand, "be dam av I wudn't like to go to his funeral!"

Chapter 8

Sobraon

During the interregnum between Aliwal and Sobraon, the main body of the Sikhs was still encamped on the opposite side of their fortified bridge. Notwithstanding their repeated defeats, they still mustered some 30,000 men, with seventy pieces of camion, added to which they held a position strongly fortified, so that our troops looked forward to having another and sanguinary encounter before the war was finished. Day by day the enemy added to the strength of his works under the direction of a Spanish engineer, while Sir Hugh Gough waited for his heavy bulldogs (artillery) and other reinforcements.

Under Sir Charles Napier, a column of 16,000 men was moving up the left bank of the Sutlej towards Ferozepore, and must have proved, had the war lasted, a most valuable aid to Sir Hugh; but Sir Charles did not arrive in time to share in the glory of Sobraon, overtaking the army at Lahore, on their return, after the battle.

The first portion of our siege train, with the reserve ammunition for 100 pieces of artillery, arrived from Delhi on the 7th and 8th of February. On the last-named day, Sir Harry Smith's division having come in, Sir Hugh resolved to commence operations at once.

Sobraon, the Sikh post, is a village on the right bank of the Sutlej, twenty-five miles from Ferozepore, and fifteen from

Ferozeshah, and all that the enemy held there of Indo-British ground was composed of their fortified camp at the bend of the river which washed the rear, while it presented a semicircular front of 3,500 yards.

Daily in our camp, every man-jack, (to use a classical expression) was getting more eagerly impatient for what Barney Hennessy called a wire in—and the more refined, a final encounter, with the enemy. Their works had been repeatedly reconnoitred by Sir Hugh Gough, who wrote: "Our observations, coupled with the reports of spies, convince us that the arduous task has devolved upon us of attacking a position armed with the most formidable entrenchments, not fewer than 30,000 men, the flower of the Khalsa troops, with seventy pieces of cannon, united by a good bridge to a reserve on the opposite bank, on which the enemy had a considerable camp and some artillery, commanding and flanking his field-works on our side."

At that point, the Sutlej, which takes its rise in a valley of the Himalayan chain, is fully four hundred yards in breadth. On the 9th February, most of the horse artillery were detailed to man the heavy guns, and the writer's troop was named for the rockets: this change of equipment from horse to foot artillery was the cause of some dissatisfaction and grumbling, at the issue of the order, but the feeling of discontent gradually wore off before nightfall. The Iron Duke used to say, "He is a fine soldier who grumbles—and goes!"

At night, we fell-in and marched off to our respective posts as foot artillerymen, full of jokes, calling each other "Old Fogs" (the old cant name for the dismounted artillery), as we marched along. We left our tents standing, our bedding and other worldly possessions rolled up in the tents, and bitterly cold we found it, without either tents or bedding. But our high spirits, and hopes of giving the enemy a sounder thrashing than they had yet had, kept us pretty well up to the mark. Barney Hennessy, was, as usual, to the fore with his, what the Dublin jackeens call humbugin, and was the cause of many a jolly laugh, either at his own or his comrades' tomfoolery. We had a man in the troop who was (or had been) a veritable foot artilleryman, but, as Barney said, "he had a fifty-seventh cousin, or uncle, or brother—or a sister bedad—who knows?" in our troop, and had procured a transfer. He was by no means a proficient in the science of equitation, and there was invariably much laughter at the manner in which he went through the motions, even the most simple, although he did his best, and had the "makins," as Darby phrased it, of a dragoon in him in time. But as matters at present stood he was infinitely more qualified for a dismounted than a mounted artilleryman.

For a couple of hours, at all events, on the night of the 9th of February, he was a hero without doubt. Barney selected him as the ground-work of his amusement, and fortunately the man himself had too much good sense to lose his temper, and show how hardly he was being hit, through the chink in his armour which Barney had discovered. The quietest horse in the troop had been placed at this man's disposal, and with even that advantage he had some, difficulty in preserving his mounted equilibrium. Everyone knew this, and however ill-natured it may appear, nothing sooner set the fellows off laughing at score than an allusion to Magann's horsemanship.

On this night, our posts having been allotted, we were chatting over the events of the day, the probable result of the morrow's operations, and shop generally, when Hennessy made his appearance at our fire, where Magann was sitting. He looked round him stealthily, the palm of his broad hand smoothing his moustache, as usual, and seating himself opposite to Magann, after "passin' the time o' night" with the others, looked earnestly and gravely at him, and said—more apparently in a soliloquy than addressing any one particular, "I knew it! He's lukin pale an' interestin'! I don't think he's at home here; he ought to be wid his chums in the ould 'Fogs'!"

"Who's that?" queried one of the group.

"Ach!" answered Barney, with an air of disgust, "who shud it be? But that wonderful horse-rider from Jucrow's[1] cirkis, Magann there!"

"Lave him alone. Barney" another would interpose, his anxious desire that Barney should continue the wheel, evinced by his manner of speaking.

"The man wants rest," said another.

"Divil a bit," said Barney, "he had rest enough when he was in the 'Fogs' to last him all his service, av it was twice 21."

"Anyhow," continued Barney, "the divil a rest he'll rest until he hears what I've got to tell him—and the rest of yez—and when he does hear it, the Lord give him good av id!"

Here, interjections of "Whist"; "Aisy;" "Spake aisy; lis'en to Barney!" "Out wid it Barney;" "Go un man;" and such adjurations, fell on the astonished ears of Magann, who had no idea of what was to be the outcome of the hubbub which Barney had raised round him.

Barney himself, slowly nodding his head at the fire, and kicking a stray ember back to its place with the toe of his boot, was softly ejaculating, still in the way of talking to himself—"Well well! The luck o' some people! There's nobody comes to me an' says Hennessy I want you to carry despatches; I'll make an ehjeconq[2] av ye! Sorra lie in id; what are ye laffin' at you Andy Brennan, wid yer yahoo look?' D'ye think I couldn't carry a dispatch as well as Magann, although he's a sintar?"

"Eh?" one fellow said—"A what?"

"Take the wool out o' yer ears," said Barney, "didn't ye hear? A Sintar"

"Musha now," said another, "that's a quare name all out! Is it Hindoostanee, or Madrassee, or Bengally, or whatee?"

"Av yer edukashin hadn't been neglected (don't be laffin, Brennan, it's well ye know radio an' writin' wasn't taught at the school you attindid), you wud know, the lot o' yez, that a sintar was the rale ould Gracian-Latin name av' a half-man

---

1. Ducrow's.
2. *Aide-de-camp.*

half-horse,—that was in the time o' the Cazars, and Magann's the best imitation av wan we have in the troop! Boys, deer, when we see him mounted, we'll think we've gone back to the dark ages!" And here the inimitable wink, the screwing up of the face into wrinkles, and the sparkling fun all over Hennessy's face, proved so contagious, that a general guffaw was the result.

"Now," said Barney, "iviry man is laffin' but Magann, an' av the truth was known he's laffin' too—but,—" and here a wonderful oscillation of the eyelid took place—"On the wrong side av his mouth! Listen to me now. Here's the story: The fame av this Magann's horsemanship has rached the chief himself; an' upon me sowl, when tomorrow's fight is over, an' we bate the Sikhs (which plaze God were goin' to do), Magann's the man to take the despatch to Ferozepore, mounted on Bancroft's horse, who will go wid him as the divil went thro' Athlone, in standin' leps! and the Lord look down on him this night!" Here there was another guffaw.

The horse in question (the writer's horse) was the terror of all timid horsemen ; he was christened the Sikh, and if ever there was a vagabond horse foaled, he was that foal. For powers of endurance no horse in the battery was his equal; he was sagacious, as knowing as a jailor, was trained to perfection: but, let your eye be off him, or your leg away from his side for an instant, he was a "desaver!" And in addition to his other qualifications, "he would," (as Barney said) "av he got the chance, ate you up wid all the composure av a New Zaylander!"

Judge, then, of the effect of Barney's declaration on poor Magann! But he wasn't finished yet. When the laugh subsided (and it was a peculiarity of Hennessy's that he never laughed at a joke of his own, or that of any one else) he was assailed by exclamations of "How dy'e know?" "Who tould ye?" "Arrah now, ye joke," and so on.

"Ah! well!" said Barney, proceeding to gather himself up, having raised a laugh, which was what he wanted, "yez are all talkin'. Joke!"

"Be this book!" (here he held up a pipe with an inch and a half of stem, and as black as a boot,): "here's the words the chafe said to the capten this day, 'Waller,' says he, 'ye have some fine men in yer troop!'

"'I have, Sur Hew,' sed the capten, lukin mighty plazed!

"'Divil a finer man ye have nor Magann, says the chafe!'

"'Tare an' ouns' says the capten, 'd'ye know Magann?'

"'Know him, is id,' says the chafe, 'bedad his mother used to wash for us ill the ould place in the Wist!'"

(Here another guffaw) "'Whisper, Waller,' says he: 'After tomorrow, I'm goin' to sind Magann wid despatches to Ferozepore, d'ye mind now! I want to do him a good turn—an' if the Sikhs don't kill him, Bancroft's horse will, and ye'll be rid av a bad bargain.'

"'Bad bargain!' sed the capten, 'ye sed he was a fine man just now.'

"'So he is,' said the chafe, givin' the capten a dig with his elbow and a wink like this—luk at me," said Barney, and he wound up his face and set it a-going amid loud laughter— "'he's a fine man to get rid av!' an wid that they parted! Magann, me deer, say yer prayers, an' mike yer will av ye haven't made it yet; an' whatever you lave me—an' God space ye to yer wife an' children, don't attimpt to lave me yer reputashin—for me own is bad enough widout yours on me back." And with a "God save ye!" Barney strode away into the night, leaving everyone laughing except poor Magann, whom Hennessy had sat upon properly!

By daybreak on the 10th, mortars, heavy guns, &c, &c, were all in position on the alluvial land within accurate range of the enemy's pickets in front, of Korleewallah, and at what was called the little Sobraon, while the disposable field artillery were also ranged in an extending semicircle embracing within its range of fire the whole works of the Sikhs. It was originally intended that the cannonade should commence with the dawn, but a dense white mist hung over the plain, the silent flowing river, the Sikh village and Chota Sobroan, and until the sun penetrated and cleared the atmosphere, showing the works of the Sikhs, prevented the intention being carried out.

The action commenced by a salvo from the guns, howitzer, mortar, and rocket batteries. Such a salvo was never heard in the length and breadth of India before, or one may venture to say, since, for it shook the very earth, and roused the Sikhs from their slumbers. Repeated salvoes were fired and the reports of the guns were distinctly heard by the wounded in hospital at Ferozepore, five-and-twenty miles away. Our lighter guns opened fire near Chota Sobraon with a battery of howitzers, and before half past six the whole of our cannonade was developed and every iron-throated gun, mortar and rocket battery—the latter served, as has been said, by the writer's own troop of horse artillery, acting as foot—was raining a storm of missiles which boomed, hissed and hurtled through the air into the trenches of the Sikhs.

We had seen a large body of the enemy's cavalry in their picturesque dress, with their standards waving, advancing at a brisk pace, apparently towards our battery. We immediately gave them a salvo of rockets, followed by single doses; the hissing noise of the long, destructive shafts, and the shells bursting unerringly among them, suddenly threw their ranks into the utmost confusion, and they were ultimately driven back in a whirlwind of defeat, leaving hundreds slain upon the field. The cavalry charged no more that day. Although nothing could be more magnificent than the manner in which our guns were served, it would have been more than human to expect that they alone, and that within a limited time, could silence a responding fire of seventy pieces of cannon behind ably constructed .batteries composed of earth, flanks and fascines, or dislodge disciplined and well trained troops, covered by redoubts and epaulements, within a triple line of entrenchments.

Our terrible cannonade made extraordinary havoc among the enemy, and torn and shattered corpses lay thick and deep around their guns, as subsequent inspection proved. But it was apparent to all that the issue of the struggle remained to be tested by the musket and the bayonet. By nine o'clock Stacy's brigade, flanked by Horsford's and Fordyce's batteries, and Lane's troop of horse artillery, moved to the close attack in magnificent order, the infantry and the cannon aiding each other co-relatively. The former marched steadily in line, with its colours flying in the centre, and halting only to close in and connect where necessary; the latter taking up their respective positions at a gallop, until all were within three hundred yards of the Sikh batteries; but notwithstanding the regularity, the soldier-like coolness, and the scientific character of the assault, which Wilkinson's brigade supported ably, so terrible was the roar of musketry, the fire of heavy cannon, and of those pestilent little guns known as *zumboorucks*, and so fast fell our dead and wounded beneath them all, that for some moments it seemed impossible that the trenches could ever be won.

But very shortly the whole of our centre and right could see the gallant soldiery of Stacy swarming in scarlet masses over the banks, breastworks and fascines, through smoke, and fire, and steel, driving the Sikhs before them within the area of their own defences, over which the yellow and red colours of the 10th and 53rd were flying; and not less gallant was the bearing of the 43rd and 59th Native Infantry, who were brigaded with them and swept on with them shoulder to shoulder! At this moment—the first of success—Sir Hugh Gough despatched Ashburnham's brigade to further support the attack, while the divisions of General Gilbert and Sir Harry Smith threw out their light troops to threaten the works, under cover of an artillery fire.

As these assaults by our right and centre commenced, the fire of our heavy guns had first to be directed to the right, and then had gradually to cease as our infantry closed in; but at one time the mighty thunder of fully 120 pieces of cannon reverberated along the plain and in the valley through which the Sutlej flows; and as it was soon seen that the weight of the whole force within the Sikh camp was likely to be thrown on the two brigades that had passed its trenches, it, became necessary to deliver close and frequent attacks with the skirmishers and artillery of the centre and right. From the latter to the extreme left flank, the battle was now raging with indescribable fury. When hurled back in various places at the point of the bayonet, the Sikhs flung themselves forward in yelling masses, and renewed the contest with sword and shield.

Nor was it till our cavalry of the left, led by Major General Sir Joseph Thackwell—a one armed officer, who had two horses shot beneath him at Waterloo—had moved forward and ridden through the openings made in the Sikh works by our sappers, apertures so narrow that they could only pass in single file and form up as they entered; and until the 3rd Light Dragoons, whom no obstacle, usually held formidable by cavalry, seemed to check, had, on this day, as on that at Ferozeshah, galloped over and hewed down the defenders of the batteries and field works; and when the full weight of three divisions of infantry, with every piece of field artillery that could be sent to their aid had all been cast into the scale, that victory was finally declared for the British. Here it was that every available horse artilleryman, who had been working the heavy guns, was ordered back to camp to bring up the light guns, which were all ready horsed for them. They, nothing loth, and delighted at the change, sprang on their horses and rattled down to the river.

The fire of the Sikhs as they fell back towards the river slackened, while the victors, horse and foot, pressing upon them, precipitated them in wedges and helpless masses over the bridge and into the Sutlej, in the waters of which there had been a sudden rise of some inches that rendered it no longer fordable. In their wild and frantic efforts to reach the opposite bank they suffered a horrible carnage from our flying horse artillery, the grape from which beat the water into bloody foam, amid which heads and uplifted hands were seen to vanish by hundreds, as they were swept away by the current.

"Hundreds fell under this cannonade," says Sir Hugh Gough's despatch "hundreds upon hundreds were drowned in attempting the perilous passage. Their awful slaughter, confusion, and dismay were such as would have excited compassion in any breast or in the great hearts of their generous conquerors, had not the Khalsa troops, in the earlier part of the action, sullied their gallantry by slaughtering and barbarously mangling every wounded soldier whom the fortune of war had left at their mercy."

Our two battalions of Gurkhas, active and ferocious Nepalese, armed with the short weapon of their native mountains, were a source of great terror to the Sikhs throughout the conflict and the subsequent flight. By eleven a.m. the battle was over, and the bridge destroyed, while seventy-seven pieces of cannon, 200 *zumboorucks*, or camel swivels, many standards, and vast munitions of war were the trophies of our victory. Among those who fell was the gallant Sir Robert Dick, K.C.B. who was mortally wounded by a grape shot when close to the 80th Regiment, and expired in the evening, thus closing a brilliant career of service which had commenced in the last year of the last century, when he joined the 78th Highlanders. His remains were buried in the cemetery at Ferozepore with military honours. Our total casualties amounted to 2,283.

The Sikhs acknowledge that they had 37,000 men engaged in this battle, and their loss on this occasion was from 13 to 14,000 men.

Five days after the action, and when the walls of the entrenchments had been nearly levelled to the ground, a sandbank in the middle of the river was completely covered with dead bodies of the Sikhs, and all the camp was strewed with the carcasses of men and horses, most of which were left as a prey for the jackal, wild dog and vulture. In this battle, as in the previous action, Prince Waldemar of Prussia was present, and was frequently seen riding where the danger was greatest. Thus, the invading Sikhs were defeated in every action with the loss of more than 220 pieces of field artillery.

For their brilliant services in the wars of India, Sir Henry Hardinge and Sir Hugh Gough were both raised to the peerage, the former as a Viscount, the latter as a Baron; Sir Harry Smith was made a Baronet, and your most obedient very humble servant was sent back to the hospital at Ferozepore, the wound he received at Ferozeshah having broken out again. A Medical Board assembled at the hospital at Ferozepore when hundreds of the wounded were invalided and sent home to England, via Bombay, and the remaining hundreds were despatched to the hills, or Umballa. The writer was fortunate enough to be among the latter.

Our mode of travelling was simple and desultory enough. Those who were very weak, and unable to knock about much, were carried in *doolies*; and those who were strong enough to walk a little and help themselves a little, were conveyed in common country carts, with a mat covering, improvised for the occasion, to shade them from the sun's rays; there were two men in each cart. The tents were pitched and struck by *doolie* bearers and lascars. Before leaving camp, every morning, we were supposed (mind you—supposed means what a Scotchman called "whether or yes," when he meant "whether or no") to have a cup of coffee per man. It was a compound of a most delectable nature; and there is no harm in saying, at this distance of time, that, like the Marchioness in The Old Curiosity shop, if you thought the beverage was coffee "you must make-believe very much indeed." If the private opinion of this deponent was requested on the subject, he is bound to say, with his hand upon his heart, that if the villainous berry from which the so-called coffee was decocted was not charred gram, it was the most accurate imitation of it he has ever tasted!

But this was not all: the refreshing nature of the "cup that cheers and not inebriates" (he supposes the quotation will apply to coffee as well as the greenest of green pekoes) may be guessed, when the reader is informed that there was neither sugar nor milk along with the decoction. "And," said Barney Hennessy, when he was told how luxuriously the sick fared of a morning, "bedad, me deer, I know all bout it! It takes a man wid an' edukashin an' experience like me to understan' thim things! It's the likes av me that knows the kind o' stuff ye got! D'ye mind now? That mornin' coffee on the line o' march—a medical comfort they called id, bekase its supposed to keep the could air out av yer stomak—the divil sweep them an' their comforts av suppositions—that mornin' coffee was just like the play av Hamlet wid Hamlet left out!"

"How dy'e make that out, Barney?" said one.

He looked at his questioner with a glance of infinite scorn, and slowly said—"Well, I thought ye had more nous. That coffee sur, was like the play this-a-way; the play is nuthin, widout the Prens o' Denmark, and is no play, thin'; an' there bein' no coffee in yer mornin' draft—the divil recave the coffee was in the mixter. Coffee! be gorra I'm glad ye found a man fur id! I could pick the gram out av the grounds at the bottom av the tay-pot any day in the week! However, ye got the stuff it was made from anyhow."

We never reached the next camp ground before noon, and about an hour afterwards we had a teapot full of the same species of drinkable with milk and sugar, and a pound of brown bread, and for dinner we had mutton—"Och!" said Barney, "mutton is id! as rank a goat as ivir climbed a rock, and a tough ould divil at that!"—either in chops or boiled, every man his pound. The extras, such as eggs, fowl, pudding, wine, &c, were not for us: we were the cart division; they were stopped the first day's march from Ferozepore. The sick who were carried in *doolies* (the *doolie* division) may have had their extras continued, but we were two distinct corps, as our mode of travelling will show. Our marches were short, say, about 10 miles a day, for the progress was slow, necessarily, never reaching beyond the wonderful rate of two miles an hour.

Our route lay over the fields of Ferozeshah and Moodkee, and those who were able walked over the ground where the battles had been fought. The areas of both fields were thickly strewed with human skeletons (all Sikhs) in hundreds; and the putrefying carcasses of horses, camels, mules, bullocks, &c, made the sight and the smell equally disgusting.

The *doolie* division had many casualties in the shape of deaths between Ferozepore and Umballa. Their bodies were interred without coffins, or even clothes, or any ceremony whatever, and many a fond mother's darling, a father's hope and pride, all that maiden or wife loved as she loved herself, found a nameless grave under the shade of a peepul or at the foot of the trunk of a mango tree—

"Unwept, unhonoured, and unsung!"

As for the cart division we didn't lose a man! It consisted of men of the Horse and Foot Artillery, 3rd Light Dragoons and 9th Lancers, and we reached Umballa on the 21st of March where the writer had the pleasure of joining his wife, who presented him with a baby of two days old—his first-born son. The child had taken a great liberty with destiny; and had independently come into the world without the leave or consent of the writer being first had and obtained. He simply appeared and asserted himself.

The writer's troop had returned from Lahore and was temporarily stationed at Ludianah, where they were located in the horse lines, their horses being picketed in the open. From thence a lieutenant (a married officer) proceeded to Umballa to bring up the soldiers' families and his own. On his arrival, the writer reported himself to him, informing him that he had found his wife unfit to travel with him to the hills, and that he had resolved to stay behind the detachment to attend upon her, accepting all the consequences which might ensue. The officer told him that he had acted perfectly right in adopting such a resolution; took upon himself the responsibility of his absence from the party; furnished him in the kindest manner with the sinews of war, and directed him to proceed with his wife and child to rejoin his troop at Ludianah.

After a few days rest at Umballa, the Writer was ordered to take with him all the women and children of the troop. Bullock carts, with mat coverings, were procured (one cart for each family) as the means of conveyance to be adopted, and off we started, travelling by night, and halting by day, protected from the almost vertical rays of the sun by the grateful shade of the immense trees, under which we bivouacked. In addition to the great heat, the hot winds were at their worst carrying on their wings blinding and choking dust. The majority of the women and children under the writer's charge were suffering from fever and opthalmia, and to mend the matter there was no medical aid. But after about, ten days of this weary work, Ludianah was reached without a casualty.

CHAPTER 9

Quarters

On our cavalcade, or bullock-cart-ade, whichever it may be termed, approaching the barracks (old stables), the writer's troop-mates turned out to a man to welcome them in. It was a joyful occasion for the wives and children whose husbands and fathers were spared to return to them again, and terribly bitter for the poor widows and orphans whose husbands and fathers had been left on the battle field. No hearty greeting and welcome waited upon them although every attention which respectful sorrow could pay them was cheerfully accorded.

As for the writer, his old ramshackle cart was speedily surrounded with willing and eager hands—Barney Hennessy at their head—preferring assistance to help his young wife and child (the latter of whom had already been received into the community by the title of the "young pay-sergeant.") This assistance was gratefully accepted, his right arm being still in a sling, and he not being able to do much in the way of helping any one just then.

"Salient, deer," said Barney, his hand over his moustache as usual, "av ye'll get the mistress an' the young paymaster into marchin' order, I'll do meself the pleasure av conductin' ye to the halls av dazzlin' light where yer goin' to be quartered. The place might be a dale better, but in these times a fellow has got to be content wid the very smallest av mercies."

With this he led us to what he termed "the staff-sarjent's quarters," consisting of two gram or store rooms, at the end of the stables! With amazing celerity, for many hands make any work light, the place was cleared out and we were soon nicely settled, and as we were meditating how lucky it was to have our troop-mates to welcome and assist us, a voice was heard shouting in stentorian tones: "Three cheers for the young pay-serjeant," which being duly given, was followed by the expected demand to drink his health and that of the "old woman"—the united ages of mother and child making 20 years! To get rid of the good-humoured mob, the writer was compelled to ask the mistress to give them a few *rupees* to drink the health of herself and her baby.

Of course she gave the money with much pleasure, and as soon as they got hold of the circulating medium they very soon had the grog, for the bagdadding system had been re-established, and was in full swing at four *annas* per dram, or in the regimental cant of the day, "four tent pegs for a mallet." The health of the young pay-sergeant, his father, and his mother, was drunk in the most outrageously hearty manner, and in point of fact, the satisfaction of the entire troop was so great that a boon day—holiday—was applied for and granted, and that done the fellows set about enjoying themselves each in their own peculiar fashion.

Thus ended the writer's campaign of the Sutlej, leaving a mark on his arm which he will carry with him to his grave. He still possesses the sleeve of the jacket he wore throughout the campaign. It was a brief, but an eventful one, and was succeeded two years later by the Punjab campaign.

Allusion has been made in these pages to shouts being raised by our fellows, when the first gun of the campaign was fired on our side, of—"There's our twelve months' batta! Hurroo, yer sowls!"

"Glory be to John, dacent man, in Leadenhall Street, there's seventy-six chips fer iviry man-jack."

"Hurroo!"

And true it was: as during the stay of the troop at Lahore it was notified that twelve months' batta would be distributed to the European soldiers, and Christian drummers, &c., of native regiments. The amount of the batta was seventy-six *rupees* per man to every European soldier, from the rank of sergeant-major downwards, and half that amount to the boys, and to the Christian drummers one hundred and twenty *rupees*;

"Makin' a differ," as Barney Hennessy remarked, "av fouran' forty chips betune a rale 'ould British, Irish, or Scotch sojer, an' a native cristen! Be what process o'rasonin';" said. Barney, "them gentry av ours, who do the rithmitical part av the fighten' and durty paper wid their scratchin' an cipherin', like an ould gander in stubble, make out that there's a differ of six an' forty *rupees* between the like av—av—av—Me!" and here Barney drew himself up to his full height, threw his chest well out to the front, and hit himself a sounding slap in the region of the torso (if a Christian drummer had had half such a thump he would have been absquatulated!) "an—an a Christian drummer!"

"I think," he continued "that I've made out many a puzzle in me time; and unravelled many a tangled skein, o' me own an' others' makin'; but such a twister as this, I nivir kem acrass! I think it's past rasonin! It can't be on account av his colour, for black is only comely, even in the daughters o' Jerusalem! and unless it is that he's been a long time in the country, the divil aknow I know what's it's fer"

Many of Barney's listeners were satisfied with his solution of the difficulty, but the glaring disparity of the reward, in proportion to the service done, and *raison d' être*, puzzled many wiser heads than Hennessy's.

The prospect of this largesse being distributed was delightful to the genus *bagdadder*. They had amassed considerable sums by their immense profits in the bartering of grog, and were eager to increase their spoils by enlarging their sphere of operations. There was some delay in the issuing of the *batta*—there always is about the conferring of a boon such as that—and such men of the troop as wished to forestall the issue, found ample scope to encourage them to do so for a consideration. They were disposed to go on a spree, could they only find the means, and Mister Bagdadder, with his money bags, was but too willing to help them. He would give them forty *rupees* for their seventy-six—there was a chance for both! An immediate indulgence for the man who wanted the money, and a sure and speedy return to the troop Shylock! There were contingencies, such as death, &c, to be sure, but these must, be risked, and the end of the matter was that bargains were effected on the above principle, and the batta changed owners. The men held their spree, while the *bagdadder* held the *batta*, and as is not uncommon in such circumstances, the hard won earnings were anticipated, and instead of them dancing to the good old tune of "money in both pockets," their frames were racked, and their whole system shattered, for the time, by over-indulgence.

But the *bagdadding* fraternity were destined not to have their own way altogether. Knowing well the squandering propensities of the men with whom he had to deal, the Commander-in-chief ordered, that in lieu of twenty-six *rupees* of the batta to be issued, a summer kit should be provided for each man, whether he wanted it or no; and thus at one fell swoop the Shylock's profit was reduced from thirty-six to ten *rupees*! Great was their consternation! And loud and uproarious was the laughter at the Nemesis which had waited on them: at the snare into which they had fallen. No blame could possibly attach to the seller, but with what pangs of deep regret the *bagdadder* saw his percentage dwindle, and six and twenty rupees wrenched from his vice-like grasp.

But they had yet another card, as Hennessy said, "in the heel o' their fist." The allowance for boots and half mounting, an allowance long since discontinued, six *rupees* per man per year, was still due. The troopers longed to cure their head, the *bagdadders* longed for fifty percent. They bought all up and when money was eventually issued, no man, save the *bagdadder*, profited aught—and even he groaned in spirit, because he did not realise expectations!

"What!" said Barney to one of the genus, who was down on his luck, and had been sowld: "what, man alive, are ye letting out your face four holes for?"

"Aisy for you to talk," said the other, "you're well off; I'm not so well off as I expected, and I risked me money!"

"Ye haythen," said Barney, "d'ye know what's in your Bible? Ye don't? The divil doubt ye! Ye poor craythur, there's a sayin' in id, that just describes yerself this minnit—'It is blessed are them that expect nothen, for they wont be disappointed.' d'ye mind, now?": and with a dig in the ribs he left him!

CHAPTER 10

Soldiering 2

1846. Ludhiana.— The troop occupied the horse stables, the horses were picketed on the common, a married man, wife and family were allotted the stall for two horses, no doors, large bamboo and mat screens to shelter them from the hot winds, dust storms, &c. One night a terrific storm came on, about, this time a great rumbling noise was heard, presently news came that all the European barracks had fallen to the ground, and several men, women and children were crushed. Her Majesty's 50th Regiment of Foot occupied the barracks, two troops of Horse Artillery (1st and 2nd Troops 1st Brigade.) marched out at night to render assistance with lanterns, and implements, worked all that night and next day—and found all the men and women and children that were crushed to death (50 men, the number of the regiment). The writer forgets the number of women and children, they were all buried without coffins in long pits dug in the cemetery, the 50 soldiers in one pit. It was a mournful sight.

1847.—The 2nd of the 1st Horse Artillery, the writer's troop, marched to a new station in the Punjab called Hooshyarpore, the troop remained in tents till the barracks were built. Here the writer's wounded arm broke out again through the heat, temperature in tents 120.

1848. At Hooshyarpore the writer's wife presented him

with another son.

1848-49.—Went on the Punjab Campaign. After this campaign the writer was admitted into hospital, he remained three months in the hospital and was reduced to a skeleton open out suffering from a severe attack of the liver, he also lost the use of his wounded arm and right leg. After his recovery the troop was ordered to march to Peshawar (40 days). Arrived at Peshawar on the 1st January 1850. The change brought the writer round to his former strength. From 1850 to 54 his troop was stationed in Peshawur. The station was very unhealthy, all the soldiers were suffering from fever, spleen and liver. The writer was the only man that had no fever, but he suffered very much from neuralgic pains in the wounded arm. All these four years he was constantly engaged against the Mohmunds and Hill tribes with the force under Brigadier General Sir Colin Campbell, K. C. B., west of Peshawur.

1852.—The present Lord Roberts joined the Regiment as a subaltern.

1854.—The writer's troop marched to Jullundur, then he was transferred to the 7th Regiment Light Cavalry on promotion. He was handed over on parade to Captain Boileau, Adjutant of the Regiment.

1855.—The writer received several injuries in the right leg and foot on duty. He was then appointed Sergeant Major to the Murree Depôt.

October 1856.—After recovering from the injuries received he was remanded to the Artillery Regiment at his own request as sergeant. He rejoined his old troop under a new designation, from Colonel Waller's to Major H. Tomb's troop, stationed in Jullundur. On arrival at Jullundur he went up to Major Tombs to report himself. On saluting him the Major made use of the following expression at first sight "I presume you are Sergt. Bancroft, you and I will never be good friends." He found fault with his riding on parade, and would have him to go to riding school and learn to ride. The writer replied, "that he could ride the tail off any horse in the troop," which he proved, by riding a horse that was resting for some time. The writer was not sent to riding school.

1857.—The troop marched to Meerut in less than a month. The writer was tried by a court-martial and reduced to the ranks and pay of a gunner. On the 10th of May, on a beautiful Sunday evening the mutiny broke out at Meerut. In the morning the artillery and the 6th Carabineers went to church. The 60th Rifles were to attend church in the evening. As the regiment was formed up there was firing heard from the native infantry lines. The native infantry were formed up and marched down to the 60th Rifle barracks to murder the women and children in the barracks, choosing the time the Rifles were in church. The European officers of the native regiments went out to see why the regiments were formed up. The sepoys shot them down, this was the cause of the firing. A gentleman galloped down through the rifle and artillery lines giving the alarm that the native cavalry and infantry had mutinied.

The Rifles ran off parade into the barracks and took up their rifles and ammunition (the writer may here add that heretofore the infantry left their guns in barracks attending church parades, and only went in side arms)—and did not attend church. The writer's troop of Horse Artillery (Major Tombs) galloped to the native infantry on parade, led by Major Tombs. On reaching them the sepoys fired a volley, the troop came about into action and opened fire with grape which soon made the mutineers run for their lives and made their way, joined by the native cavalry, into Delhi. The officers' bungalows and the mess houses were on fire. Ladies and gentlemen who attended church were murdered on their way home. If the mutineers had been followed up by the troop of horse artillery, a squadron of the 6th Carabineers, and a company of the 60th Rifles, some of them seated on the artillery wagons, Delhi would not have fallen into the hands of the mutineers. The mutiny would have ended. There were quite enough troops left to look after Meerut. It is hard for the writer to say where the fault lay.

1857-58-59.—The writer was constantly engaged with the enemy,—see the writer's record of services at the end of the book.

1858.—On the 5th May the writer's only brother was killed by his side, a cannon ball went through his right breast. Sir Henry Norman was present at the storming of Bareilly where the writer's brother was killed. The troop returned to Meerut.

1859.—Lieutenant-Colonel J. H. Smythe, C. B. returned off leave from England, and commanded his old 5-1 Horse Artillery (natives) out at a place called Philibeet. He allowed his sergeant-major to retire from the service and recommended him for a commission. The sergeant-major declined the offer, he received instead the highest pension that could be got, *viz*: 2s. 6d. per day and an annuity of £20 per year for life.

Then the colonel asked the sergeant-major how he could be replaced?—the sergeant-major replied "you must have heard of Bancroft, who was pay-sergeant for twelve years, also sergeant-major in Colonel Waller's troop, well he is a gunner in the same troop in Meerut—and called Colonel Tombs—you had better send for him."

Colonel Smythe being the senior regimental officer present he commanded the 1st Brigade Horse Artillery temporarily. He sent the following order to Meerut: "Gunner Bancroft to be promoted to sergeant-major and transferred from the 2-1 to 5-1 Horse Artillery, and to be sent when a force was marching in that direction towards Bareilly or Moradabad,"— Colonel Tombs sent for Gunner Bancroft and asked him if he was ready to join his new troop, the gunner replied he would be in a few days.

The colonel replied, "if you are not ready in a week's time

you shan't go at all."

The writer replied "I am ready now."

He was ordered to be settled up with, receiving a balance of Rs. 5. His sword was taken from him, he was provided with a cow-cart to carry his bedding at his own expense. The following day the writer marched out of Meerut with a walking stick for protection. It took the writer from the 18th of January to the 8th of February to reach his new troop out in an enemy's country.

On arrival the writer called at Colonel Smythe's tent to report his arrival. The colonel came out of his tent and said, "I presume you are Sergeant Major Bancroft, have you had any breakfast?"

The writer replied that he had been living on sweets and hand cakes purchased in the bazaars for the last twenty days.

The colonel called for Major Renny and told him to take the sergeant major to the mess and get him a breakfast. After breakfast he returned to the colonel's tent. The colonel spoke very kindly and said that he had just come in time to have another brush with the enemy,—this news pleased the writer.

The colonel then said "My Sergeant-Major has retired from the service and gone to England, and if you serve me as truly and honestly as you did Colonel Waller for twelve years: I and you will be good friends, and I will allow you *Rs. 60 per mensem* in addition to your pay, and further, I have brought you away from your greatest enemy Colonel Tombs, his ambition was to disgrace you by scratching your back. I returned to my tent and in a few days we had a brush with the enemy at Sissyah and Maylaghat on the banks of the Sardu River near Philibeet, from thence the troop returned to Moradabad, and Colonel Smythe returned to England.

In Moradabad the troop got another commanding officer, Colonel H. Hammond and marched into Meerut, where the native troop was broken up, and a European troop was formed bearing the same designation 5-1 Horse Artillery in 1860. The writer finished his 21 years service in the Bengal

Horse Artillery.

1861—The troop volunteered for the British army, and the writer volunteered to serve five more years in the F. Battery, C. Brigade, Royal Horse Artillery, See appendix, notes 4, 5, 6 and 7 for the testimonials given by the different commanding officers under whom the writer served.

1862.—The troop marched from Meerut to Cawnpore, there the troop got another commanding officer, Lieutenant-Col. H. Le G. Bruce. (Colonel Hammond left on promotion). The troop then marched to Allahabad, from there to Lucknow, where the colonel left on promotion. Then the troop got another commanding officer, for a short time, in Captain Sir William Hamilton.

1865.—The writer lost his wife in Lucknow. The whole troop including officers attended the funeral.

1866.—The troop marched to Benares, where the writer obtained his discharge, under the command of Major G. R. Brown.—See record of service.

Chapter 11

Pay and Stoppages

Before I conclude my narrative I will give you in detail how the soldiers of the Old Bengal Horse Artillery were paid, fed, and clothed, just to show the vast difference between them and the soldiers of the present day; the condition of the latter is better known to the reader, perhaps, than to the writer.

The pay of the gunner was   *Rs.* 14. 6. 8.

Monthly stoppages.

Extra messing and servants   *Rs.* 7. 3. 0.
2 drams of rum per day   ,,   3. 3. 8
                                 ,,   10. 6. 8.
Balance, all told   *Rs.* 4. 0. 0.

Rations per day.

Bread 1 lb; beef 1 lb in the summer and 1½ lb in the winter, a pinch of dirty salt, and 3 lbs all told of fire-wood.

Clothing: and stoppages for same;

1 Dress jacket, biennially, of the very worst description blue cloth, trimmed with yellow braid, with 99 brass buttons, scarlet cuffs and collar; 1 pair of coarse Oxford mixture overalls, with a single yellow stripe down the sides, biennially.

1 Pair of buck-skin breeches, or pantaloons, of good qual-

ity biennially.

1 Pair long boots (or *Rs.* 5 instead) annually.

1 Pair jack spurs (steel) once for all.

1 Pair white leather gloves, annually.

1 Cloak (more like an overcoat) of coarse blue cloth, triennially.

1 Brass helmet, triennially, with a leopard skin turban and a long red horse-hair mane flowing down the back: all but the helmet to be paid for!

1 Silk girdle, (yellow and red stripes) by paying for the same.

1 Stable jacket, cap, a pair of Wellington boots and a pair of brass spurs, all to be paid for.

Half mountings for alteration of clothing, Annually	*Rs.* 1	0	0
Placed under stoppages for fitting the clothing	*Rs.* 10	0	0
Stable jacket, cap, boots and spurs	*Rs.* 15	0	0
A summer kit	*Rs.* 25	0	0
Total	*Rs.* 51	0	0

Besides the above stoppages a recruit on joining his troop was made to pay his share towards mess tables, forms, mess utensils, copper boilers, and provide himself with a cot and box: I leave you to guess how long a recruit was under stoppages, having only *Rs.* 4 of a monthly balance to pay off all his debts

The luxury of a *punkah* in barracks was not known in those days.

Bedding,

A coarse chintz quilt, with about 3 lbs of cotton stuffed into it, was issued annually, and before the quilt was in use a month the cotton got lodged all at one end of it.

I will further inform my readers, that on the line of march all soldiers were placed under stoppages for the carriage of their bedding, at the rate of one camel to every eight men, which amounted to *Rs.* 8 per month between the eight men, and the marching and campaigning in those days generally lasted for a lengthened period, there being no railways in India, and still, on the whole, the Old Bengals were a happy and contented race of beings. After all their shortcomings, they were full of life and spirit, and were always ready when required.

The following are the names of the officers under whom the writer had the honour of serving from the time he was first transferred from the Bengal Foot to the Bengal Horse Artillery, in 1841 to 1846, the end of the Sutlej Campaign;

Captain F. Brind, Comdg. 1-3 H. A.
Lieutenant C. V. Cox, 1-3 H. A.
Lieutenant F. B. Boileau, 1-3 H. A.

1st Brigade B H A,

Major General Sir G. Pollock, C. B., Comdg,
Lieut-Col. C. Graham, C B,
Lieut-Col. G. Brooke, C B.
Lieutenant John Anderson, Adjutant and Quarter-Master.
Surgeon T. E. Dempster, Medical charge.
Assistant Surgeon John Murray, 2-1 H. A.
Captain G. S. Lawrenson, Comdg. 2-1 H. A.
Captain and Brevet Major E. D'Arcy Todd, K. L. S., Comdg., 2-1 H. A.
Captain and Brevet Major R. Waller, Comdg. 2-1 H. A.
Lieutenant E. Christie, 2-1 H. A.
    "   "   W. K. Warner, 2-1 H. A
    "   "   H. Apperley, 2-1 H A.
    "   "   C. A. Wheelwright, 2-1 H. A.
    "   "   W. A. Mackinnon, 2 1 H. A
    "   "   H. P. de Teissier, 2-1 H. A.
    "   "   C. Blunt, 2-1 H. A.
    "   "   S. C. Woodcock, 2-1 H. A.

Appendix A

MEDICAL CERTIFICATES

I hereby certify that Sergeant Bancroft, 2nd-1st Bengal Horse Artillery, has frequently been under my treatment for severe neuralgia pains in the right arm. I believe these pains are unduly dependent on injury to some branches of the brachial plexus caused by a cannon-shot.

Sergeant Bancroft was wounded by a cannon-shot at Ferozshuhur, and he has been subject to these pains ever since. They are usually aggravated by changes of weather and derangement in the hepatic or dejective visclea.

(Sd.) J. G. Kemp M.D.
Assistant-Surgeon,
Horse Artillery
Peshawar: December 1853.

I hereby certify that Quarter-Master Sergeant Bancroft, late of the 7th Light Cavalry, has suffered much during the two last hot seasons from acute neuralgia pain of the right arm which was extensively lacerated by a gun shot wound, in the battle of Ferozshuhur, and he states that since the date of injury he has suffered more or less every succeeding hot season. I am therefore of opinion that a change to a hill climate may be attended with great benefit in this case, and were he to remain in the plains his general health could not fail to be undermined; but by a residence of two or three connective years in the hills his health would be improved, and further tendency to neuralgia symptoms removed, when, with the permission of Government, he might be enabled to rejoin the more active branch of the service, and under this opinion (given by me) Quarter-Master Sergeant Bancroft has been induced to resign his present appointment in the 7th Cavalry.

In September last Quarter-Master Sergeant Bancroft, when on duty received a severe injury of the foot by his horse falling, and he is only now recovering from the effect of the accident.

(Sd.) M. McNeill, Rind,
Surgeon 7th Cavalry
2nd January 1856

Military Certificates

No 1.

Certified that I have known Qr.-Mr.-Sergt. N. W. Bancroft, of the 7th Regiment, Light Cavalry, late Staff Sergeant of the 2nd Troop, 1st Brigade Horse Artillery, for the last ten (10) years mid upwards, during eight years of which he was Pay-Sergeant; I always found him to be a smart, zealous Non-Commissioned Officer, of considerable firmness and determination with Europeans, well acquainted with all his duties, and uncompromising in the performance of them. From an intimate knowledge of this character and disposition I consider him well qualified in every respect to fill either of the situations of Sergeant-Major or Quarter-Master-Sergeant of the Convalescent Depôt, Murree. He was severely wounded in action at Ferozshuhur, and although it has not interfered with the execution of his duty, he has often suffered from the effects of it during the hot weather.

(Sd.) R. Waller, Lieut.-Col.,
Commdg. 2nd Troop, 1st Bde., H.A.
Jullunder: 27th August 1854

Copy of Office Records

No 2.

I recommend Quarter-Master Sergeant Nathaniel Bancroft for the situation of Quarter-Master Sergeant of the Murree Convalescent Depôt; he bears an excellent character, he reads and writes well, and is a good accountant. He is a man of sober and temperate habits, and has been most attentive to his military duties since he joined the 7th Light Cavalry, on the 21st January 1854. He has served on the Sutlej Campaign, was present at the actions of Moodkee, Ferozshuhur and Sobraon, in the second of which he was wounded in the arm by a round shot, from the effects of which (though not interfering with the performance of his duties,) he suffers much during the hottest seasons of the year.

He has received the Sutlej Medal and clasps, served in the Punjab Campaign of 1818-54 against the Mohmunds in the Peshawur Valley under Sir Colin Campbell, K. C. B., Medal and Clasp.

(Sd.) J. Mackenzie, Lieut-Col.,
Commdg. 7th Regl., Light Cavalry.
(True Copy.)
(Sd.) R. A. Master, Lieut.-Col.,
Commdg. 7th Light Cavalry.

No. 3.

From what little I have seen of Quarter Master Sergeant Bancroft during the period (six months) I have been in command of the Regiment, I have much pleasure in recording my opinion, and acquiesce in the description of the character and acquirements as stated in the preceding extracts from the records in the Regimental Office.

(Sd) R. A. Master, Lieut. Col.,
Commdg. 7th Light Cavalry.
Jullunder: 31st July 1864

No. 4.

Quarter Master Sergeant Bancroft has served in my Battery nearly four years as Pay-Sergeant and Quarter-Master Sergeant. Throughout the whole of this period he displayed the greatest zeal and attention to every duty; his exemplary conduct, excellent abilities and soldier like habits, rendered his services most valuable. On leaving the Battery, I have much pleasure in writing the above, and trust it may prove useful after his retiring from the service.

(Sd.) J. Percivall, Capt., R. H. A.,
Commanding F. C. R. H. A.
Lucknow 31st July 1864

No. 5.

Quarter-Master Sergeant Bancroft, served under me in F. Battery, C. Brigade, Royal Horse Artillery for upwards of 3 years, I cannot speak too highly of him; he is the best Non-Commissioned Officer I have ever known during my service; he is active, intelligent, most trustworthy, an excellent writer and accountant—a good horseman. As an Agent or Steward to look after property, he would be invaluable, in fact I know of no situation he would not fill with credit to himself and advantage to his employer. I can most confidently and strongly recommend him.

(Sd) H. Le.'G. Bruce, Lieut. Col.
Late Commdg. F. C. R. H. A.
Lucknow: 30th May 1865

No. 6.

Quarter-Master Sergeant N. W. Bancroft was Quarter-Master Sergeant of my Battery from September 1859 till the date of my leaving it in 1862; during this period hie fulfilled the duties of his position and also those of Pay-Sergeant in a manner which I have never seen equalled since I have been in the service. Quarter-Master Sergeant Bancroft, in addition to having very good abilities and being an excellent manager, and understanding the native character, is a thoroughly trustworthy and honest man.

His intention is to leave the service and try to obtain some appointment in India, in which, should he succeed, he will, I am certain, give the utmost satisfaction to those who may employ him.

It gives me much pleasure to be aide to give this certificate to Sergeant Bancroft, and I shall be very glad to hear of his obtaining some suitable employment.

(Sd.) H. Hammond, Col.
Commdg. Det. C. Bde., Horse Arty,
Lucknow: 31st October 1866

No. 7.

I have much pleasure in expressing the high opinion I formed of Quarter-Master Sergeant Bancroft during the year and a half I was with him in F Battery, C. Brigade, R. H. A.

For nearly nine months of that time I was in command of the Battery, and had the best opportunity of knowing how he performed his duties.

There was in both 1864 and 1865 much extra work from the equipment of the Battery being entirely changed, and it was therefore of importance to have some one as Quarter-Master Sergeant, who not only knew his work but could be trusted. I always found him most careful in saving useless expenditure. I am aware that previous to my joining the Battery, he conducted the whole of the office work and pay; and it was only on a change of system being ordered that I confined him to his peculiar duties as Quarter-Master Sergeant, Every one in the Battery will, I am sure, be happy to learn that he has obtained employment, and I will be glad to do what I can to assist him in obtaining something to do.

I trust, however, he will not have to wait long for an appointment,

Sd.) Wm. Hamilton, Capt.,
Royal Horse Artillery.   Benares: 13th March 1866

Appendix B

Major E. D'Arcy Todd, K.L.S.
(Late Political Agent, Herat)

Elliot D'Arcy Todd arrived in India as a 2nd Lieutenant of Artillery in May 1824; served with the Fort Artillery at the siege, and capture of Bhurtpore in 1825 26; was attached to the Horse Artillery early in 1826, and continued with that branch until April 1833, when he was appointed by Lord William Bentinck to the British detachment serving with the disciplined troops of the Shah of Persia, and was employed on various duties, civil and military, in different parts of that country, from 1833 to 1838, under Sir John Campbell, the Right Honourable Henry Ellis, and Sir Ellis and Henry Bethune, to the last mentioned of whom, he acted as Military Secretary.

In 1836 he was promoted, by his late Majesty William the Fourth, to the local rank of Major in Persia, having the year previously received from the king of Persia, the order of the Lion and Sun. In 1838 Major Todd was appointed to officiate as Secretary of Her Britannic Majesty's Legation at the Court of Persia, and in that capacity accompanied His Excellency Sir John McNeil to the Persian Camp before Herat; from Herat he proceeded, in May 1838, to India, via Candahar, Cabool, and the Punjab, with despatches from Sir John McNeil to the Governor-General, who was then at Simla. In October

1838, Major Todd was appointed Political Assistant and Military Secretary to the Envoy and Minister proceeding from Shah Shooja to Cabool, and accompanied His Majesty from Lodiana and Shikarpore.

Major Todd was afterwards employed as Political Agent with the Bombay division of the army of the Indus on its march from Larkhana on the right bank of the river to Candahar. Shortly before the army left Candahar, en route to Cabool, Major Todd was appointed Envoy to Herat, and proceeded with several engineer and artillery officers and a supply of treasure to that city. The city of Herat, which had withstood a siege of nine months against an enemy of thirty thousand Persians, was reduced to a heap of ruins, when Mahomed Shall retreated from before the place in September 1838 The mission under Major Todd reached Herat in July 1839? at this time there were not more than four or five thousand inhabitants in the city, and these were principally the military retainers of the King and Chiefs. To bring back the people to their homes; give them the means of cultivating their fields; to encourage trade; to conciliate the various chiefs dependant on the Government of Herat, and to establish an useful influence in the country by every means in his power, were the principle duties on which Major Todd was employed, and that his proceedings at Herat were met with the unqualified approbation of his superiors. Such is the outline sketch of this officer, who afterwards fell at the battle of Ferozshuhur, whilst commanding the 2nd Troop 1st Brigade Horse Artillery.

A marble tablet is placed to his memory in the Dum Dum Church. The following is a copy of the inscription:—

> Sacred to the Memory of Capt., E. D'Arcy Todd, K.L.S.
> Who, after a zealous service in many responsible situations, fell at the battle of Ferozshuhur,
> On the 21st December.
> Whilst commanding the 2nd Troop 1st Brigade Horse Artillery.

Aged 38 years.

In him the distinguished corps to which he belonged lost one of its brightest ornaments,

And the Church of Christ upon earth a devout and humble worshipper.

This Tablet is erected by his sorrowing relatives, by whom he was much loved,

As a slight tribute of affection.

"We sorrow not even as others which have no hope; for them which sleep in Jesus will God bring with Him. 1st Thes., 4., 13, 14."

Appendix C

By the English mail that arrived in Simla on the 6th February 1900 a private letter was received by me (the A.A.G., R. A) from Sir Arthur Bigge, saying that the rules and conditions of the Diamond Jubilee Medal were such that not eligible to receive it.

But that the following outlines of services were placed before Her Most Gracious Majesty the Queen Empress, who was much interested in the story of your long and gallant career and has been most graciously pleased to bestow upon you the medal of the Victorian Order, and also to present you with a framed photogravure likeness of herself as she appeared in the Diamond Jubilee procession, with her autograph thereon. I am rejoiced at being able to give you such good news, and most heartily congratulate you. This is a personal decoration Her Gracious Majesty gives occasionally and which you are at liberty to wear in civil life.

In the mean time Sir Arthur Bigge desires me to obtain from you, as it is Her Majesty's wish, with a photograph of yourself, and information why you live in Simla and whether you have any appointment in Simla. In accordance with the expressed wish of Her Most Gracious Majesty will you please send me the photograph of yourself at the present time, and with it give me a copy of the book of your service in detail, and the information as to why you live in Simla and if you hold any appointment here.

1.—Reply. To why I live in Simla? After serving the Government 55 years, the latter 22 years I served in Calcutta in charge of the Lunatic Asylum for which I received a second pension, and my son holding the post of Superintendent in the office of the Director General of the Indian Medical Service brought me and my wife to Simla in 1888 to live with his family in the one house. In 1890 my wife died in the house. In 1897 my son died in the same house. During the summer months I remain with my late son's family.

In the winter months I go down to the plains visiting the different branches of the Army Temperance Association.

2nd.—Reply. To if I hold any appointment in Simla?—I am a member of the Governing Council of the Army Temperance Association of which His Excellency the Commander-in-Chief of India is President, which is proved by the paper On Guard of February 1900.

14th February 1900—Received the following from the A.A.G. R A.: I thank you for your letter and the A.T.A. paper On Guard. I have sent them both away to Major Boileau, H. A., the Secretary of the R. A. Institution Woolwich, to be forwarded on to Sir Arthur Bigge for Her Most Gracious Majesty's information. Now I want a copy of your photograph for the R. A. Institution, Woolwich. I also would like please another copy of On Guard of February 1900, and a copy of your book to enable me to ask some body in a position worthy to present you with Her Most Gracious Majesty's personal gifts, and thus place the officer in possession of the history of your life and the cause of these presents to you,

OUTLINES OF SERVICES.

1. That I entered the service of the Honourable East India Company in the distinguished Regiment of Artillery on the 1st February 1833.

2. That I was present on parade, as a soldier, in 1837, when the salute was fired announcing the accession to the throne of

Her Most Gracious Majesty the Queen.

3. That my first Campaign was in the year 1838, in Jodpur, which was practically a bloodless one, but it entailed considerable exposure, hardships and privations, being carried on during the monsoons—On the troop engaged—For this Campaign no honours were awarded.

ALSO FROM LEONAUR
AVAILABLE IN SOFTCOVER OR HARDCOVER WITH DUST JACKET

A JOURNAL OF THE SECOND SIKH WAR by *Daniel A. Sandford*—The Experiences of an Ensign of the 2nd Bengal European Regiment During the Campaign in the Punjab, India, 1848-49.

LAKE'S CAMPAIGNS IN INDIA by *Hugh Pearse*—The Second Anglo Maratha War, 1803-1807. Often neglected by historians and students alike, Lake's Indian campaign was fought against a resourceful and ruthless enemy-almost always superior in numbers to his own forces.

BRITAIN IN AFGHANISTAN 1: THE FIRST AFGHAN WAR 1839-42 by *Archibald Forbes*—Following over a century of the gradual assumption of sovereignty of the Indian Sub-Continent, the British Empire, in the form of the Honourable East India Company, supported by troops of the new Queen Victoria's army, found itself inevitably at the natural boundaries that surround Afghanistan. There it set in motion a series of disastrous events-the first of which was to march into the country at all.

BRITAIN IN AFGHANISTAN 2: THE SECOND AFGHAN WAR 1878-80 by *Archibald Forbes*—This the history of the Second Afghan War-another episode of British military history typified by savagery, massacre, siege and battles.

UP AMONG THE PANDIES by *Vivian Dering Majendie*—An outstanding account of the campaign for the fall of Lucknow. This is a vital book of war as fought by the British Army of the mid-nineteenth century, but in truth it is also an essential book of war that will enthral.

BLOW THE BUGLE, DRAW THE SWORD by *W. H. G. Kingston*—The Wars, Campaigns, Regiments and Soldiers of the British & Indian Armies During the Victorian Era, 1839-1898.

INDIAN MUTINY 150th ANNIVERSARY: A LEONAUR ORIGINAL

MUTINY: 1857 by *James Humphries*—It is now 150 years since the 'Indian Mutiny' burst like an engulfing flame on the British soldiers, their families and the civilians of the Empire in North East India. The Bengal Native army arose in violent rebellion, and the once peaceful countryside became a battleground as Native sepoys and elements of the Indian population massacred their British masters and defeated them in open battle. As the tide turned, a vengeful army of British and loyal Indian troops repressed the insurgency with a savagery that knew no mercy. It was a time of fear and slaughter. James Humphries has drawn together the voices of those dreadful days for this commemorative book.

AVAILABLE ONLINE AT
www.leonaur.com
AND OTHER GOOD BOOK STORES

www.ingramcontent.com/pod-product-compliance
Lightning Source LLC
Chambersburg PA
CBHW022007100426
42738CB00041B/725